THE MIRACULOUS POWER
OF BILLY GRAHAM

What power does Billy Graham possess that has made him America's greatest spiritual awakener —helping literally millions to ease their anxieties, relieve their doubts, and find peace and salvation?

Is it his wisdom? His intense love of God? His deep human sympathy for the frailties and follies of humankind? His shining vision of what people should and can attain and achieve?

In part, it is all these things. But even more important is *his power to communicate*. No other figure of our time has his ability to take the sacred truths of the Scriptures and put them in such a way as to make them instantly alive within all of us. No other evangelist has driven the divine message home with such irresistible inspiration.

In this remarkable collection of the best of Billy Graham, his voice comes through crystal clear to every reader—a message of understanding between God and man.

MORE CHALLENGING READING
FROM YOUR FAVORITE AUTHORS
Complete and Unabridged

BLOW, WIND OF GOD!

Selected Writings of
BILLY GRAHAM

Edited by
Donald E. Demaray

SPIRE BOOKS

Fleming H. Revell Company, Old Tappan, New Jersey

A SPIRE BOOK

Published by The New American Library, Inc.,
for the Fleming H. Revell Company.

First Printing (Spire Edition), April, 1977

Grateful acknowledgment is made to the following publishers,
publications, and individuals for permission to reprint those writings of Billy Graham copyrighted by them: Chicago Tribune-
New York News Syndicate; *The Christian Century* (The Christian Century Foundation); *Christianity Today;* Doubleday and
Company; Billy Graham; *Look* (Cowles Communication); *Nation's Business* (The Chamber of Commerce of the United
States); Fleming H. Revell; Van Kampen Press; and Zondervan
Publishing House. For complete information on the source of
each reading in this book, see pages 117-121.

All Bible quotations are from the King James Version unless
otherwise indicated. Scripture passages from the Revised Stan-
dard Version (RSV) © 1946, 1952 are used by permission of the
Division of Christian Education of the National Council of the
Churches of Christ in the United States of America. Passages
from *The Living Bible* (LB) © 1967 by Tyndale House Publishers, Wheaton, Illinois; those from *The New English Bible*
(NEB) © 1961, 1970 by the Delegates of the Oxford University
Press and the Syndics of the Cambridge University Press; and
those from *The New Testament in Modern English,* translated
by J. B. Phillips (Phillips), © 1960 by The Macmillan Company, New York.

This is an authorized reprint of a hardcover edition published
by Baker Book House.

ISBN: 0-8007-8307-7

Contents

Foreword

This book of readings has been a long time in forming. At least fifteen years ago the idea was suggested by Richard Baker, son of the founder of Baker Book House. The thought has never left me, and while the project has presented formidable obstacles, I have found joy in pursuing it. Now that the task is completed at last, I put away my marking pencil with a tinge of sadness, but also with a great sense of excitement. I am excited as I anticipate that the truth of the gospel will succeed once more in the business of nurturing Christians-in-the-making.

Historians tell us that 1949 was the turning point in the evangelistic career of William Franklin Graham. It was my privilege to see the 1949 Los Angeles crusade firsthand. I was a student at the University of Southern California and attended several of those tent meetings in the southern part of the city.

How well I remember the university students' mostly skeptical reactions. One said, "How could any man give that many 'lectures' and be good at them all?" (The crusade, planned for three weeks, ran to eight!) Another commented, "I'll wait and see what I believe about this man called Graham."

In a student news sheet, a writer made fun of the "circus-tent" evangelist and asked the question of ministerial students, student pastors, and future religious leaders, "How are we to act and react when the 'tent' comes to town?"

But others were more sober. Evangelicals experi-

enced great satisfaction; those wanting desperately to
see the forces of righteousness win lifted praises to
God.

It was precisely at this time that J. Edwin Orr came
to our university. He lectured to an eager audience in
the philosophy building. At the close of that lecture, I
had the privilege of talking to him—my first conversation with the man who later became a close friend—
about overseas study. Shortly thereafter, I had my initial firsthand exposure to European and British
thought. Since then, I have returned repeatedly to England for study in some of the most remarkable li-
braries of the world.

Orr, widely recognized as the chief authority of our
day on revivals and their history, spoke ten minutes
one night at the Graham crusade in Los Angeles. His
pungent arguments against those who flatly deny the
eternal truth came right through to the intellectually
oriented. It was somewhat amusing to see the short Dr.
Orr alongside the towering young Graham. Graham
looked for all the world like a center on a basketball
team!

At the same Los Angeles campaign, Henrietta
Mears, director of religious education at Hollywood's
First Presbyterian Church, spoke briefly one night.
Billy introduced her with warmth and enthusiasm, and
well he might! Only weeks before, Miss Mears had had
him and Orr at a camp in the mountains of Southern
California. At that time Orr spoke nightly on the work
of the Holy Spirit, and issuing from that series of talks,
Graham and others experienced a new touch of the
Holy Spirit, apparently the touch that made the Los
Angeles crusade history.

What history! An inroad into the underworld; a con-
tact with the radio industry for which Hollywood is
world-renowned. But especially battles here and battles

there, until hundreds—most of them ordinary and un-known—had been won for the Lord Jesus.

The Graham movement was off, and the years ahead would see creative evangelistic thrusts through radio, publications, television, movies, and spiritual counseling.

Crusades grew in size—the Los Angeles Colosseum; the campaign in Japan of which Graham said, "It was one of God's surprises"; and the massive Korean thrust with its unbelievable attendance on the final Sunday afternoon. These are, of course, but examples of an astonishingly expanding ministry.

With growth in numbers has come growth in spiritual power. I rode one evening with Robert Ferm of the Graham Association from Winona Lake, Indiana, to a Chicago airport. Bob commented on the noticeable increase in the divine power of Graham's preaching, citing the Boston campaign as an illustration. Ministers of the gospel who had worked in Boston for years watched hardened sinners, men they quite frankly never expected to yield to Christ, come down the aisles and make forthright decisions.

How does one account for all this? "Organization," say some. But surely that is only an instrument, not the central cause. The answer is one word: *God*.

God works, said William Cowper, an eighteenth-century English poet, in "mysterious ways his wonders to perform." Graham would seem an unlikely candidate for the high and divine position he holds. But the fact is, he is the chief evangelist-prophet in the world His training, however, is not in theology; his B.A. from Wheaton College is in anthropology! He was a farm boy converted in his teens, and he was a Bible school student in Florida before enrolling at Wheaton.

He is heard by many people not only in auditoriums and amphitheaters, on TV and radio, but also through the printed word. In fact, the medium of the printed page has peculiar advantages, most particularly the leisure to meditate on what is being said.

Here, then, in a book of readings, we have the chance to meditate on such fundamentally important matters as prayer, piety, and the practice of our faith in a broken world. We have the further opportunity to think about Christ, His cross and resurrection, His power and the many-faceted salvation He offers. Billy's total faith in the inspired Scriptures to guide and motivate is everywhere seen, and a special section exposes vividly his belief about the Bible.

Billy is unafraid to plow right in to the moral issues of our day. Thus the readings on sex, marriage, and family; on guilt, worry, fear and loneliness—and identity, too—on hostility, temper, dissatisfaction and cynicism.

The Holy Spirit, His infilling and power, could not help but find an important place in such a book as this. God's love, care, and holiness are discussed as well.

Graham's perspective on money (do we spoil our children with it?), tithing, and spending gives plenty of food for thought.

The church, with its problems and potential, comes in for its share of provocative analysis, as does the Christian life and the whole business of overcoming our hang-ups.

Billy Graham—God's prophet of the day. Read him thoughtfully and therefore with profit.

Preface

For Christians-in-the-making, this book of Billy Graham readings comes to grips with the development of a strong and genuine Christian life.

The spiritual genius of Graham's writing and preaching is that Christ is always absolutely central. Get into right relationship with Him, and while your problems are not magically solved, you are at last on a sound and solid footing for handling those hang-ups. In other words, a Biblical perspective emerges, and that perspective brings hope, contributes to building steel-like character, and makes joyous living an exciting possibility.

Seasoned Christians will want to read this book for their own profit, then pass it on to younger Christian friends. All will benefit from Graham's pungent analyses of our times. Students of Graham will be reminded once more of his ability as a Christian communicator, an ability that can be summed up in two words: *simplicity* and *authority*. Always he speaks so a child can understand; always he speaks with the Bible as his authority.

But there is still another significant factor in his communication—the inspiration of God's Spirit. "Sometimes I have quite literally stepped back to let the Holy Spirit rush by," said Billy Graham in a public meeting, "and it has seemed on these occasions that I could almost hear and feel the rushing of the mighty wind of Acts 2."

Yes! In his messages one can "hear and feel" the

"mighty wind," and that is precisely why this book is entitled *Blow, Wind of God!* Those words come from Henry H. Tweedy's moving hymn, "O Spirit of the Living God." The second verse reads:

> Blow, wind of God!
> With wisdom blow
> From mists of error, clouds of doubt,
> Which blind our eyes to thee!
> Burn, winged fire!
> Inspire our lips
> With flaming love and zeal,
> To preach to all thy great good news,
> God's glorious commonweal!

So it is that when Billy preaches and the wind of God blows, His Spirit moves on a street crowd in the ghetto, on students at Harvard, on a great crowd of London preachers, on a massive audience in the Los Angeles Colosseum.

It seems not to matter *to* whom Graham speaks, only *for* whom.

William Franklin Graham has spoken to more people than any preacher in church history. He is the first evangelist since the apostle Peter to see as many as two thousand come to Christ in a single service.

Clearly the Spirit of God "blows" through his preaching and writing.

It is my fervent prayer that God's Spirit will blow through these readings, bringing sinners to repentance, nurturing believers in the eternal faith, resurrecting a keen sense of hope in apprehensive hearts, stirring the church to effective soul winning, and helping to make young Christians throughout the world strong, stalwart followers of Christ akin to the first-century disciples we read about in the Acts of the Apostles.

DONALD E. DEMARAY

1

The Holy Spirit

Filled with the Spirit

I want to ask you something. Are you filled with the Holy Spirit?

... it is time to be filled with the Holy Ghost. The secret of the power of the early church was the Holy Spirit. "Not by might, nor by power, but by my spirit, saith the Lord."

I want to ask you something. Are you filled with the Holy Spirit? Let's confess it. We're not filled with the Holy Spirit. Therefore, everything we do has a question mark about it. If you are not filled with the Holy Spirit, then the things that you say and the decisions you reach may be led by the Spirit, or they may not be. You may be totally wrong in your whole life unless you are filled by the Spirit, and moment by moment led by Him. You are not a victorious Christian unless you are filled with the Spirit. You cannot be used of God unless you are filled with the Spirit.

What is to keep us from shaking our world for Christ? Only one thing—failure to be filled with the Holy Ghost!

We have a greater opportunity today than Paul ever had. I imagine if Paul can look down here, he is "champing at the bit." How he would like to be on television! How he would like to have a radio hour! How he would like to get on a plane and go from Corinth to

Rome. How he would like to use some of the facilities
we have for saving the lost.

Paul isn't here, but we are! God is depending on us.
But we are not willing to pay the price. We are stymied
by our love of ease and pleasure, and by our pride.

The Spirit of God Lives in You!

> ... the Spirit of God dwelleth in you. (I Cor.
> 3:16)

... the Spirit of God lives in you! Before He ascend-
ed into heaven, Jesus Christ said: "And I will pray the
Father, and he shall give you another Comforter, that
he may abide with you for ever; even the Spirit of truth
... ye know him; for he dwelleth with you, and shall
be in you" (John 14:16, 17). During His lifetime,
Christ's presence could be experienced by only a small
group. Now Christ dwells through His Spirit in the
hearts of all who have received Him. The apostle Paul
wrote: "... the Spirit of God dwelleth in you" (I Cor.
3:16). The Holy Spirit is given to you, not for a limited time, but *forever!* Accept this fact by faith!

The Unpardonable Sin

> ... he who blasphemes against the Holy Spirit
> will not be forgiven. (Luke 12:10 RSV)

As with all Scripture, you need to see the situation
in which Christ made this remark. The Pharisees, those
enemies of His, had just attributed His good works to
the powers of darkness and evil. Now, this accusation
was no chance one, such as might be the result of im-
pulse or compassion. Those who accused Him knew

better. It came from a super love of self. The Pharisees had seen Christ teach, not once but often. They knew that every word and work of Christ was holy and pure. In order to accomplish their selfish ends, however, they denied what their own hearts told them was the truth. They "quenched" God's Spirit.

It is this kind of total and violent denunciation of God's Son that blocks out any possibility of personal salvation. Obviously, if you deny the Forgiver, there is no forgiveness.

In the work of evangelism, you seldom mention this because the "unpardonable sin," as it is called, is not characteristic of most people in an audience. In fact, the number who have thus sealed their doom is probably extremely small. But it does warn all of us to guard against any trifling with God's Spirit.

The Power of the Holy Spirit

> There is a divine mystery about Revivals. God's sovereignty is in them. (*Alexander Whyte*)

At times I did not need to preach. After testimonies by some of the converts, all I needed to do was to give the invitation. One night, midway through the message, a man ran down the aisle and asked if he could be converted right then. He had been standing outside the tent, fighting an inward battle with the devil. Conviction of his sin so filled his heart that he could not bear to wait until after the meeting to make his decision. That sermon was never completed as God prompted me to give the invitation right there. . . . I have never in all my life seen men and women under such conviction of sin as in the Los Angeles campaign.

The Holy Spirit Will Help

... you often will have a conflict within.

Now the Bible teaches that the moment you come to
Christ you become engaged in a great conflict. "For the
flesh lusteth against the Spirit, and the Spirit against
the flesh: and these are contrary the one to the other:
so that ye cannot do the things that ye would" (Gal.
5:17). This means that you often will have a conflict
within. True, you do possess a new nature, you have
been born from above, but the old nature is still there.
Now it is up to you to yield to the reign and control of
the new nature which is dominated by Christ. The
Holy Spirit will help. Before you came to Christ, you
practiced sin. In other words, sin was your habit. You
were dominated by sin. Now that power has been broken, and the Bible teaches that whoever is born of God
does not practice sin (I John 3:9). You may fall into
sin, but you will immediately be sorry. You will hate it.
When you, as a Christian, commit a sin, you will be
miserable until the sin is confessed and fellowship with
God is restored. The difference between the non-Christian and the Christian is that the non-Christian makes
sin a practice; the true Christian does not. The latter
abhors sin and tries to live by the commands of God
with the help of the Holy Spirit. Thus, Paul describes
Christians as those "who walk not after the flesh, but
after the Spirit" (Rom. 8:4). Again, "Neither yield ye
your members as instruments of unrighteousness unto
sin: but yield yourselves unto God, as those that are
alive from the dead, and your members as instruments
of righteousness unto God" (Rom. 6:13).

A Time for Self-examination

Is every known sin of your life confessed—
even the motives behind your actions?

This is a time for self-examination. Is every known
sin of your life confessed—even the motives behind
your actions? Are all the words that you speak Spirit-
directed? Are you tender, gracious, courteous, loving?
Are you courageous in giving your testimony for the
Lord Jesus Christ? Are you filled with the Spirit?

I ask myself that question today, "Billy Graham, are
you filled with the Spirit?" My only claim to power is
the Holy Ghost. Without Him whatever I do is of the
energy of the flesh and will be burned up before the
judgment seat of Christ. I don't care how big the
crowds are and how big the reported results are; it's all
"sounding brass" and "tinkling cymbal" unless I am
filled with the Holy Spirit.

Let us all ask the Spirit of God to sweep in upon us;
to cleanse us from all unrighteousness; to make us
Spirit-anointed and Spirit-filled men, so that God can
use us for such a time as this!

Rely Constantly on the Holy Spirit

Just relax and rest in the Lord.

... rely constantly on the Holy Spirit. Remember
that Christ dwells in you through the Holy Spirit. Your
body is now the dwelling place of the third person of
the trinity. Do not ask Him to help you as you would a
servant. Ask Him to come in and do it *all*. Ask Him to

take over in your life. Tell Him how weak, helpless, unstable, and unreliable you are. Stand aside and let Him take over in all the choices and decisions of your life.

It is impossible for you to hold out in your Christian life—but He can hold you. It is very difficult for Him to hold you if you are struggling, fighting, and striving. Just relax and rest in the Lord. Let go all those inner tensions and complexes. Rely completely on Him. Do not fret and worry about important decisions—let Him make them for you. Do not worry about tomorrow— He is the God of tomorrow. He sees the end from the beginning. Do not worry about the necessities of life— He is there to supply and provide. A true victorious Christian will be free from worries, inner conflicts, and tensions. In perfect reliance on the Holy Spirit, you will find that many of your physical and mental ailments disappear.

Supernatural Power Without the Fullness of the Spirit

. . . Jesus came and spake unto them, saying, All power is given unto me in heaven and in earth. Go ye therefore, and teach all nations, baptizing them in the name of the Father, and of the Son, and of the Holy Ghost. (Matt. 28:18, 19)

We are attempting to have supernatural power without the fullness of the Spirit. Jesus said: "All power is given unto me in heaven and in earth. Go ye therefore, and teach all nations. . . ." (Matt. 28:18, 19) In other words, we are sent forth to do a supernatural job, and don't think it is not a "supernatural" job. Winning a man to Jesus Christ cannot be done apart from the Spirit of God. The Spirit of God does the convicting; the Spirit of God does the regenerating; He does the pleading. It is the Spirit of God who brings a man to accept Christ, not you. You are only a witness and a channel. We are trying to do the work of the Holy Spirit without supernatural power. It cannot be done!

The Fruit of the Spirit

It is impossible to produce the Christ-life without the fullness of the Holy Spirit.

Now turn to Galatians 5:22. "But the fruit of the Spirit is love, joy, peace, longsuffering, gentleness, goodness, faith, meekness, temperance. . . ." That is the fruit of the Spirit, and you and I are doing our very best to produce that fruit. For a long time I tried. I tried, and tried, and tried. I struggled and struggled and struggled—I did like Paul in Romans 7. I wanted to do good, but evil was present with me—there was a raging conflict all the time and I had no victory. You know why? Because the fruit of the Spirit can't be worked up. It can't be brought about by men or women in their own strength. It is by the power of the Lord Jesus Christ in the form of the Holy Spirit which He has given us that produces this fruit. It is impossible to produce the Christ-life without the fullness of the Holy Spirit. It cannot be done! You may try to do so. You may work your fingernails off; you may work day and night to try to produce love, but you will never produce genuine love without the Spirit of God. You may try to have peace and try to be calm under all circumstances, but you will never produce peace without the Spirit of God. You may cry and plead to have joy in your life; you may run from pleasure to pleasure, attend many social events, and read books which you believe will bring joy. But you will never have real joy outside the Spirit of the living God because He alone produces joy. You may want patience and say, "Lord, control my tongue. Lord, I don't want to fly off the handle. I don't want to tell people where to get off." You will never have victory until the Holy Spirit gives you the victory.

Something Dangerous

> . . . I, brethren, could not address you as spiritual men, but as men of the flesh, as babes in Christ. (I Cor. 3:1 RSV)

I want to say something very dangerous. Did you know that it is possible to work for the Lord and live an exemplary life without being filled with the Spirit? It says concerning the Corinthians that they came behind in no gift (I Cor. 1:5-7). But Paul called them carnal Christians (I Cor. 3:1). This means that I can have the gift of an evangelist. I can get up and preach and still not be filled with the Spirit. I shall preach without power and my preaching will be as sounding brass and tinkling cymbal. You may have the gift of teaching a Sunday school class. You can have the gift without being filled with the Spirit. Because you can get up and talk or teach the Bible does not necessarily mean that you are filled with the Spirit. What an awful thing that is!

I have asked God if there were ever a day when I should stand in the pulpit without knowing the fullness and anointing of the Spirit of God and should not preach with compassion and fire, I want God to take me home to heaven. I don't want to live. I don't ever want to stand in the pulpit and preach without the power of the Holy Spirit. It's a dangerous thing.

Members of the Church
Filled with the Holy Ghost

When we join hands and the gospel is preached under the anointing and power of the Holy Ghost, revival comes. . . .

Wouldn't it be great to see the members of the church filled with the Holy Ghost? They will be if revival comes. ". . . ye shall receive power, after that the Holy Ghost is come upon you. . . ." (Acts 1:8). Not only will the church members be revived, but many more will accept the Lord Jesus Christ.

Fourteen years ago, down in the city of Charlotte, North Carolina, the ministers of our town forgot their differences; the laymen, together with the ministers, held a city-wide evangelistic campaign. Do you know one of the things that attracted me? I saw the people who, a few days before, had been quick to argue with one another, now joined together around the cross of Jesus Christ. I said, "If that is taking place, there must be something to Christianity." I went to the services and was converted in an old-fashioned revival meeting just like this. When we join hands and the gospel is preached under the anointing and power of the Holy Ghost, revival comes and souls will turn to believe on the Lord Jesus Christ.

2

Sex

Sexual Liberties While Engaged?

> No temptation has overtaken you that is not
> common to man. God is faithful, and he will not
> let you be tempted beyond your strength, but
> with the temptation will also provide the way of
> escape.... (I Cor. 10:13 RSV)

*Question: "My fiance and I are trying our best to
live the Christian life. What limit, if any, do you suggest for an engaged couple in terms of liberties taken
with each other? Thus far, we report no loss of control,
but it's a real fight."*

Answer: The matter you mention has many ramifi-
cations. It involves the whole area of self-discipline.
Some years ago, the noted psychologist Ruth Stang observed that a large number of young people were
showing interest in learning to resist the pressure of de-
linquent ideas. She and other leaders are saying that
there's a movement now toward accepting moral and
legal responsibility for one's actions. That's good, because a nation cannot last long when this is abdicated.

Perhaps the length of your engagement should be
shortened to conform with your impatient love. In any
event, pray for wisdom, treat each other with respect,
and remember the extra power that I Corinthians 10
offers: "The wrong desires that come into your life
aren't anything new.... and no temptation is irresistible.... trust God.... He will show you how to escape
temptation's power...." (LB)

Premarital Sex?

> . . . God made us to handle sexual involve-
> ment within the confines of marriage.

I am fully aware that some today would say to disregard limits on conduct under most circumstances, but
certainly if the couple plans a subsequent marriage.
The evidence, however, in emotional traumas, lingering
guilt, and a prematurely jaded life all dictate to the
contrary.

Christian or not, God made us to handle sexual involvement within the confines of marriage. Addition-
ally, as a follower of Jesus, you have the high standards of conduct that doing the Father's will implies.

Homosexuality

> Such reformation is possible for you. Seize it
> while there's still a chance.

*Billy Graham gives sound advice to a girl who says
quite bluntly, "I am a girl, and I love another girl!"*
First, let's get the text of that reference from Paul.
He wrote, ". . . Make no mistake: no fornicator or
idolater, none who are guilty either of adultery or of ho-
mosexual perversion. . . . will possess the kingdom of
God" (I Cor. 6:9, 10 NEB). These classes of sins
were especially prevalent at Corinth, where impurity of
mind and body was typical of the local Aphrodite cult.

Now all of these are developments of the same un-
godly spirit of self-gratification. Today, the appeal to
unrestricted sex and unlawful use of sex is felt every-

where. Experimentation in sexual perversions is admired.

But, let me say this loud and clear! We traffic in homosexuality at the peril of our spiritual welfare. Your affection for another of your own sex is misdirected and will be judged by God's holy standards. You know such conduct would not have been tolerated a decade ago. Because morals have so eroded, however, it is now applauded. But you don't have to succumb to this insidious temptation. Said Paul, "Sexual sin is never right."

Read on in that chapter. You will discover that the people guilty of such sin were converted—were regenerated by faith in Christ. Such reformation is possible for you. Seize it while there's still a chance.

Sex Placed Before American Young People

> Have mercy on me, O God, according to thy steadfast love; according to thy abundant mercy blot out my transgressions. Wash me thoroughly from my iniquity, and cleanse me from my sin! (Ps. 51:1, 2 RSV)

Look at the problem of sex. Everywhere, but especially emphasized and underscored here [Los Angeles], we see sex placed before American young people. If we want to sell even a motor-car tire, we have to use sex to do it. As a result, our high-school and college young people are going to the dogs morally—encouraged by the press and radio across this nation. We need a revival!

3

Marriage

Common-law Relationships

I have yet to meet anybody who made a mistake by loving and forgiving.

Distressed parents write Billy Graham: "We have a son who is living in a common-law relationship, and he knows we do not approve. We have told him we don't want that girl in our house. Since he won't come without her, we never see him. The Bible says, 'Shun the very appearance of evil,' so we feel this is the right attitude. Otherwise, he might think we favor such a situation. Are we wrong?"

Notice the loving, forgiving spirit of Billy's answer:

I believe you are wrong. The Bible says, ". . . if a Christian is overcome by some sin, you who are godly should gently and humbly help him back onto the right path, remembering that next time it might be one of you. . . ." (Gal. 6:1, 2 LB)

Obviously, your son is in love with, or at least enamored of this woman. While misled and in error, yet he values that relationship above a visit with you. You have maneuvered yourself into a corner and psychologically locked your boy out. It could only engender bitterness.

The Lord set a good example in His treatment of the adulteress who represented the opposite morality from His own. He understood her problem, not only forgave her but rehabilitated her, and taught a lesson to the

Pharisees who were eager merely to punish her wrongdoing.

When the Bible says that love never fails (I Cor. 13:8), it means it. Here's a good opportunity to check it out. Without condoning his wrongdoing, show extra love at this time—for both of them. I have yet to meet anybody who made a mistake by loving and forgiving.

Communication in Marriage

> What I'm saying is that when a couple lives
> for each other and together for God, their com-
> munication at every level is improved.

Good communication is a prerequisite for a happy marriage.

Here's a definition of *communication* from the book *American Marriage* (Crowell, 1959; p. 248): "Good communication means simply that husband and wife express their thoughts to each other, and that each is ready to listen, understand and respond."

The Bible is very clear about the basic attitude each spouse is to have toward the other. Paul said in Ephesians 5:28 that husbands should love their wives "as part of themselves" (LB). Peter had this concise advice in I Peter 3:1, "Wives, fit in with your husbands' plans. . . , your godly lives will speak to them better than any words" (LB). I know these are lofty goals, but faith in Christ opens the door to a divine power for accomplishing them.

What I'm saying is that when a couple lives for each other and together for God, their communication at every level is improved. They have the patience, the tolerance, the interest, the love needed to lead harmonious lives.

When a spiritual maladjustment is corrected, you're then able to approach other problems—successfully.

I Forgave . . . But I Can't Forget

> . . . I will be merciful toward their iniquities,
> and I will remember their sins no more. (Heb.
> 8:12 RSV)

*Here's an all-too-typical question: "We had a happy
marriage for twelve years, with three fine healthy children. Then suddenly I discovered my husband was
being unfaithful. We considered divorce, but when he
repented, we decided to give it another try. I forgave
him all right, but I can't forget. Can you help me?"*

Graham's answer is forceful:

The act of infidelity is so destructive that Christ
made it the sole reason for divorce (Matt. 5:32). Even
if a society condones extramarital activity, it does not
lessen its damaging effect on the whole family unit.
God made us, and He knows the limits beyond which
we cannot function as whole and happy persons.

But now your husband has evidently recognized all
this, and I judge has given no subsequent cause for
concern. If a couple can restructure their relationship,
after some disruption, all involved will be better off.
Getting a divorce or a separation may seem momentar-
ily attractive, but it is at best a poor solution.

Have you maintained good and open communication? This is needed to allay future suspicion and, more
importantly, to eliminate any reason for disenchantment.

The wonder of God's forgiveness is that He couples
it with forgetting as well (Heb. 8:12). He can help
you to do the same. The question is, Are you flexible
enough to adjust now, and do you have sufficient trust
to maintain compatibility? I agree that the relationship
is not the same as it was prior to his involvement. But

it can be better if both of you want it to be and will work at it.

Stepping Out on My Wife

> . . . they should repent and turn to God and perform deeds worthy of their repentance. (Acts 26:20 RSV)

A husband writes Graham as follows: "I was reared in a Christian home and was active in church until about three years ago. For some reason, then we started to drift away. To make matters worse, I have started stepping out on my wife. I know it's wrong, but it's become an obsession with me. Please say something to help me."

Graham gives a prophetic word:

Your drifting away from church was merely a symptom of a prior drifting away from Christ. Unless there is a real personal faith prompting church attendance and service, no motivation is enough to hold against the stresses of modern life.

The phrase you used, "I know it's wrong, but. . . ," is one I have heard many times. It's the giveaway for someone who has faced a temptation and has decided to yield to it, but wants to keep up moral appearances. There's nothing I can say to help you unless you desperately want to be helped.

In that case, the secret is the same for all who seek God's forgiveness and strength. Acts 26:20 says it is simply repentance and faith in Jesus Christ. Plenty of men have faced the same temptation you have—to explore extramarital relationships. But with the help of God, they've decided it's not worth damning the marriage, destroying the home, dooming yourself, and deserting the children.

While there is still time, throw yourself on the mercy of God. He will help you to stop immediately all those contacts which are ruining your life.

The Importance of Marriage

If we confess our sins, he is faithful and just, and will forgive our sins and cleanse us from all unrighteousness. (I John 1:9 RSV)

A wife asks her important question this way: "I was foolishly persuaded that in the Bible people got married by just 'taking' a wife, without bothering with a wedding. I permitted this informal arrangement, although I knew it was wrong. Later I married the man. Now, my conscience bothers me. Can I get forgiveness, or will God always hold it against me?"

Graham speaks with both authority and sensitivity:

I congratulate you for the sensitivity to wrong that prompted your letter. Unfortunately, our society seems less and less inclined to tolerate any rules on marriage.

Let me first, however, comment on what you call the Bible method of "taking" a wife. According to the original divine purpose, marriage was ordained of God and not to be entered into lightly. In fact, of the three great events in life—birth, marriage and death—marriage was thought the most important in the eastern society of the Bible. Jeremiah 7:34 speaks of a wedding procession; and, of course, our Lord's first miracle was at a marriage feast.

Never did the idea of "taking" a wife exclude societal or parental approval. In fact, the selection of the wife and the arrangement of contractual and financial matters was decided upon by the parents or guardian, never the bride and groom. Even betrothal, among the Jews, was regarded as binding as the later marriage itself. I am saying that matrimony was not ever to be a frivolous passing fancy.

As for your question regarding forgiveness, John has the answer in simple terms: ". . . if we confess our sins to Him, He [Christ] can be depended on to forgive us. . . ." (I John 1:9 LB).

Move ahead with your marriage, confident that God not only forgives the past, but provides wisdom for the present, so that marital success can be achieved.

Adultery

> . . . if you fill your heart and life with the truths of God and service to others in the name of Christ, your anxieties will be minimized, if not completely eliminated.

A distressed woman writes: "I am a wife and mother and I have committed adultery. I have prayed to God for forgiveness many times, but this sin still bears on my mind, almost constantly. I have thought about going to a psychiatrist, but I know that God is the only One who can help me completely. What can I do?"

Graham begins by quoting Hebrews:

What the Bible says about God in Hebrews 8:12 should encourage every penitent. The Lord there promises: ". . . I will be merciful to them in their wrongdoings, and I will remember their sins no more."

Consider this analogy. To light a room, we don't give a second thought about getting rid of the darkness. The switching on of the bulb automatically takes care of that. Likewise, if you fill your heart and life with the truths of God and service to others in the name of Christ, your anxieties will be minimized, if not completely eliminated.

God says He not only forgives those who have a repentant spirit and trust His Son as Savior, but He forgets that any charge was ever placed against them. God sees the believer, then, through the merits of Christ, and that means perfection. So if God forgets, shouldn't you?

Now, it must be said also that sometimes God employs means to accomplish His purposes. Not with our salvation, of course, but sometimes with our mental or physical well-being. If you do consult a psychiatrist, use that service as supplemental to the primary work of God's healing Spirit in your life.

4

The Family

Phasing Out the Family?

God gives the desolate a home to dwell in. . . .
(Ps. 68:6 RSV)

Psalm 68 has this statement: "God setteth the solitary in families." It's another indication of the divine origin of the family.

Some of the arguments for phasing out the family are made to sound plausible and even advisable. Tragic, however, are the consequences to a child when this is done. If we think there is already a high rate of emotional disease in our country, phasing out the family unit will only trigger even more monumental disorders.

The Bible has no alternative to the family. It provides ample comment for repairing it—none for eliminating it.

An Illegitimate Child

. . . there is no such thing as free sex.

Listen to this complicated question: "My nephew is accused of fathering a child by a woman who has other children born out of wedlock. He has since married a fine lady, a widow, who also has a child. This nephew believes he is wrong if he does not support that first child, and maintains it says that in the Bible. I maintain that he is wrong and that his money should go to his immediate family."

Billy answers humbly and Biblically:

I am not a competent judge in such a matter and certainly am not familiar with the laws of your state.

I think your nephew should be commended for sensing a moral obligation. The fact that this other woman bore several children with doubtful paternal origin does not prove that the child he supports is not his. If it is, or if he is uncertain about it, I believe he is under obligation to provide support. An innocent child should not be the victim of adult mistakes.

The Bible says, ". . . whatsoever a man soweth, that shall he also reap" (Gal. 6:7). This man is recognizing that he broke man's law and God's, and that he must face the consequences.

This is precisely what concerns me about the free-wheeling sex standards of today. In the very nature of things, there is a penalty for disobeying the laws of God. I think it's obvious that there is no such thing as free sex. A cost is attached, any way you look at it. How good it is when we learn that sex and family affairs, conducted as God intended, bring no grief to anyone. Rather, they provide happiness for all involved.

Family Interpersonal Relationships

A family without government is like a house without a roof, exposed to every wind that blows.

A grandmother asks a very real question: "I have had a wonderful relationship with my son, his wife, and their two-year-old daughter. I love them all dearly. Re-

*cently, in a stubborn spell, the little girl wouldn't allow
her mother and me to dress her. I held her, forced her
clothes on, and got her ready. Now they are angry with
me, and I'm afraid this incident has come between us.
Please help me."*

Billy says some important and helpful things:

What happened seems like an insignificant incident,
but perhaps it pointed up a broader and deeper disagreement over how to bring up children.

Here's one situation where the generation gap is
most obvious, but you must realize that raising that girl
is not your responsibility. Logically and legally, they
are the boss in setting standards and in determining
conduct. Grandmothers are important, but they are
never to replace the function of parents. Letting go is
hard!

Evidently, you were a disciplinarian, and your son
knows it. There's no need to continue to prove it. He
will have to develop his own philosophy of family discipline, because as Matthew Henry put it, "A family
without government is like a house without a roof, exposed to every wind that blows."

More importantly, however, I'm concerned about
what you're doing to settle the disagreement. The Bible
says in Ephesians 4:26, "Don't let the sun go down
with you still angry. . . ." (LB). Your duty is to make
peace, to ask for forgiveness—if that's involved—and
to build harmony. With the innate wisdom that God
gives mothers, you'll know how best to accomplish
that.

An Effective Testing Ground

. . . fathers, provoke not your children to
wrath: but bring them up in the nurture and admonition of the Lord. (Eph. 6:4)

*Here's a realistic family problem: "My husband and
I are in our forties. We have seven children, of whom
five remain at home. One of these is our eldest, a son,
age 24. My husband resents this boy deeply, feeling he
should be out on his own—not dependent on parents
for support. How can a man, calling himself a Christian, have such a miserable attitude?"*

Billy's answer follows:

One of the most effective testing grounds for the
Christian faith is the interpersonal relationships of the
family. If Christian principles work there, they will
anywhere.

The apostle Paul had this advise in Ephesians 6:4,
". . . fathers, provoke not your children to wrath: but
bring them up in the nurture and admonition of the
Lord." Heeding that counsel would seem to eliminate
such things as resentment, hostility, and callousness.
Young people mature at different ages, and peer
pressure from friends will often do more to develop
self-sufficiency than parental orders.

It doesn't sound like there's much communication
between father and son. Maybe that's the first place to
repair the relationship. Understanding and acceptance
arise out of a spirit of sharing.

Have your husband reread the story in Luke 15 of
the prodigal son. Tell him to note especially the attitude of the father. There's a lesson in that equal to the
one on the lost boy. I tell you, if God treated us the
way we often do others, heaven would be a deserted
place.

Radicals

> . . . he arose and came to his father. But while
> he was yet at a distance, his father saw him and
> had compassion, and ran and embraced him and
> kissed him. (Luke 15:20 RSV)

*A dad cannot understand why his son talks of quit-
ting his job and overthrowing the government.*

Billy says this:

. . . let me comment on your son. If he extols unem-
ployment and proclaims the overthrow of the government, he's been hooked by a delusion. I once talked to
a leading radical in New York City. When I asked
what he would do after burning down the establish-
ment, he told me he didn't know. His plan was only to
demolish, not to develop.

The only thing you as a father can do is to emulate
the father of the prodigal in Luke 15. He kept his love
strong and his hope high. The Scripture says that when
the boy was a long way off, ". . . his father saw him
coming, and was filled with loving pity and ran and
embraced him. . . ." (LB)

Set a good example yourself and use massive doses
of love and understanding.

The Child and His Home

> There is no institution like the family to turn
> children into civilized human beings.

It's interesting to me that in the Genesis account of
creation, the husband and wife were supernaturally
created at a mature age. The child in the first family
unit, however, was conceived and grew up in the environment of a home. God's order from the beginning

has been the family structure, and we tamper with it at great peril to all society.

Recently, in a popular magazine article this statement appeared: "There is no institution like the family to turn children into civilized human beings." We can experiment with communal living, group parenthood, solo parents, and governmental rearing of infants, but all such plans can never be equated with the norm of a father and a mother in a loving and intimate home relationship.

TV Programs and Twelve-Year-Olds

> . . . whatsoever things are true, whatsoever things are honest, whatsoever things are just, whatsoever things are pure, whatsoever things are lovely, whatsoever things are of good report; if there be any virtue, and if there be any praise, think on these things. (Phil. 4:8)

A concerned mother asks: "On all sides there is criticism today of TV programs. I am particularly concerned about the effect of violence on my twelve-year-old boy. Got any suggestions on how to handle it?"

Billy replies this way.

I am aware that the President's Commission on Pornography disputed the fact that such material has a proven bad effect on subsequent behavior. Nonetheless, I think we can easily make a case for our actions often being triggered by the things we hear, read, and observe. You do well to be concerned over the prevalence of violence in current movies and TV productions.

One editorial in the *St. Louis Post Dispatch* relates to this matter. A team of brain chemists at the University of Tennessee made some interesting discoveries about violence in the rodent family. Apparently, mice which were allowed to see other mice fighting began to show these same characteristics an hour and a quarter later. Mice which had not seen this fighting remained quiet and peaceful. Now, I'm not developing some rigid thesis on such limited investigation, but other studies also seem to show that violence begets violence.

The apostle Paul in Philippians 4 suggested that the followers of Christ major in things that are "true," that is, good, right, uplifting, spiritually edifying, and character building. While you can't monitor all your son's programs, you can counsel with him periodically about his sense of values and moral principles.

Childless?

> Lo, sons are a heritage from the Lord, the fruit of the womb a reward. Like arrows in the hand of a warrior are the sons of one's youth. Happy is the man who has his quiver full of them! ... (Ps. 127:3-5 RSV)

"I am married to a good husband," begins a concerned wife, *"but he doesn't want any children. I do. I am twenty-seven and soon will be too old to have children. I was told that you can't get to heaven if you don't have children. I need some advice. Childless forever?"*

Graham gives sound advice:

If the qualifications for going to heaven are as you suggest, then the apostle Paul wouldn't have made it. He never married!

No, I'm glad to tell you that God has made the entrance requirements for His kingdom just as simple as possible. Peter says in I Peter 1:4 that those born again through repentance and faith are made members of God's family and even receive the "priceless gift of eternal life" which is "kept in heaven" (LB).

Now on the matter of children, that's a personal decision you two will have to make. Your husband should know, however, that even the proponents of zero population growth do not suggest all couples remain childless. After all, how would the race continue? Perhaps a minister or trained counselor can help you share the reasons for your differing views. I find it personally difficult to imagine life without the benefit, the consolation, and, yes, the challenge of children. There is a sense of fulfillment and completion that comes when a husband and wife become a father and mother.

Have your husband ponder the words of Psalm 127:3-5.

Raising a Family

> Fathers, do not provoke your children to anger, but bring them up in the discipline and instruction of the Lord. (Eph. 6:4 RSV)

To raise a family in this godless age is a tremendous and fearful responsibility before God! You ought not take it lightly—it is a heavy responsibility.

Treat your children with love and understanding. It isn't always necessary to whip a child. If you have won and deserved the love and respect of your children, a spoken word is often all that is necessary. Do not give harsh commands to your children. And never make a promise to a child if you do not intend to fulfill it.

And When He Is Old . . .

> Train up a child in the way he should go: and when he is old, he will not depart from it. (Prov. 22:6)

What about you as a parent, as a dad, as a mother? Scripture says, "Train up a child in the way he should go: and when he is old, he will not depart from it"

(Prov. 22:6). That is the Word of God. If you train your children, pray for them, and live a Christ-like life before them, God says, "Though they may be wayward now, some day they will come back."

In Dad's Steps

> . . . a child left to himself brings shame to his mother. (Prov. 29:15 RSV)

There was a man who always stopped on his way to the office for a drink of whiskey at the corner tavern. There had been a snowfall the night before and on this particular morning he heard something behind him. When he turned around, there was his little seven-year-old boy, stepping as closely as possible in his father's tracks.

"Son, what are you doing? You go back home. You'll catch cold."

The little boy said, "I'm just stepping in your tracks, Daddy."

The father went to the corner saloon but something stopped him that morning. He went to his office, but he could still hear "Stepping in your tracks, Daddy." Then he began to think. I love my little boy and he loves me; he wants to follow in my steps, but my steps are leading him to hell. The father dropped to his knees and accepted Jesus Christ as Savior. Then he made this promise: "I'm going home to be an example to my little boy."

5

Money

I Wanted to Give

". . . whoever gives to one of these little ones even a cup of cold water because he is a disciple, truly, I say to you, he shall not lose his reward." (Matt. 10:4 RSV)

Beggars were all around in Bombay—some with their legs gone, others with arms eaten by disease, and blind men everywhere—all asking for money. It was one of the most heartbreaking scenes that I had seen since leaving Korea. I wanted to give every one of them the message of Christ and to give them all money. I did give some of them money.

The missionaries and others, and even the Indian leaders, had warned us already not to give money, because every time you gave a rupee (which is worth only about twelve cents but is a day's wage in India) you attract a thousand others because the word gets out quickly. It's a most difficult thing to turn your back on such poverty as this. Some may be able to do it, but I can't. I gave as many rupees as I possibly could to as many people as I saw in need. However, the missionaries and Indian leaders were right—we soon collected a great crowd who were begging and screaming and fighting for the money. We hastily got in our car and drove off.

Tithing

Bring the full tithes into the storehouse, that
there may be food in my house; and thereby put
me to the test, says the Lord of hosts, if I will
not open the windows of heaven for you and
pour down for you an overflowing blessing.
(Mal. 3:10 RSV)

*A young couple just about decided they couldn't
tithe—a look at the checkbook that's not realistic.*

Billy says:

I believe the discipline of good stewardship is one of
the little known secrets of victorious Christian living.

For one thing, you need to read again the advice of
Dr. Luke in chapter 12 of his gospel. In verse 34 he
said, ". . . where your treasure is, there will your heart
be also." So many people assume the reverse to be
true. They think when they get sufficiently charged up
with charitable emotions, then they'll give to the work
of Christ. This verse says that emotion and interest will
follow the deliberate investment of monies, not precede
it.

Furthermore, if giving to the work of the Lord is
based on some arithmetic or logical basis of salary dis-
tribution, it will never survive if it ever starts. Tithing
has to begin with love—and continue by faith.

Go ahead, try tithing and try God! Malachi 3:10
says you can't lose.

Money and Our Children

Since God made us to be originals, why stoop
to be a copy?

*A distressed father wonders at the ingratitude of his
son after putting him through school until he had his
master's degree.*

Billy's answer shows insight.

Your son may be the victim of an affluent society.
Having had such an emphasis on material wealth, on
achievement and status, many a young person has been
turned off. Having had their fill of a success-oriented
culture, they adopt a life style which is just the opposite, to demonstrate their disenchantment. Sometimes, children discover after marriage that they are no
more than puppets on the family stage; that is, they
have never been permitted to be themselves, but just a
carbon copy of their parents. Someone once asked,
"Since God made us to be originals, why stoop to be a
copy?"

A Christian View of Spending

. . . first they gave themselves to the Lord and
to us by the will of God. (II Cor. 8:5 RSV)

*Question: "Right about now every mail delivery
brings me unhappy bills for the articles I so happily
charged last Christmas. What is a Christian view of
spending money?"*

Answer: The best Bible reference for you to check
is II Corinthians 8. Paul is praising some Christians
who had a generous heart and who seemed to

represent the right attitudes in stewardship and money management.

The primary thing he noted was that "first they gave themselves to the Lord" (v. 5 RSV). It seems to me this is basic. This helps you evolve the philosophy that everything belongs to God in the first place, and you are the owner of nothing. You become a manager, trying to do the wise thing with another's property.

Selfishness, which is the essence of sin, is ever with us. It shows in the way we spend money and in other habits. Only a complete yielding to the Lord can ever conquer it.

Another facet of the problem is trusting God to provide your needs—with what remains after ten percent is given to the church and related Christian organizations. A Christian view of spending implies not only the avoidance of foolish expenditures, but the cultivation of regular giving to the work of God.

I congratulate you on your sensitivity to this matter. Giving the Lord control of the pocketbook is a giant step toward the happy possession of all of life.

Making a Quick Buck

"When the Spirit of truth comes, he will guide you into all the truth. . . ." (John 16:13 RSV)

A disturbed businessman asks his question this way: " 'To sweeten the pot' is an expression I'm sure you understand. Well, recently I've been involved in a few shady deals—but all for the sake of giving my family a better life. I'm afraid, however, that while my financial pot is being sweetened, my reputation is going sour. Why can't I wink at this the way I used to?"

Billy's forthright answer is worth careful attention:
The work of the Holy Spirit in the life of the be-

liever, according to John 16:13, is to guide Christ's followers into truth. Often, such revelations shock us, showing us the error of our ways and the need for repentance and faith. Evidently, you are being bothered by an aroused conscience which if sparked initially by divine guidance, is always a good guide to right conduct.

You are one of many today who have fallen prey to the idea that the end justifies the means. You have further been deluded by thinking that money and materialism can get your family the "good life." Once when Jesus met a man who had made a similar god of his assets, He told him to divest himself of all he had and simply follow Christ. What He was suggesting was not the poverty of being financially broke, but the riches of living for God and putting spiritual things first.

The energy crisis has produced many changes in our lifestyle which we might not have desired. All of them are not bad, however. If it gets us back to basics and back to ultimate issues in life, it will have some redeeming value. If this "crisis" you are going through shows you the value of a family where each lives for the other and all for the Lord, it will be very worthwhile.

Is Tithing Obsolete?

. . . every beast of the forest is mine, the cattle on a thousand hills. (Ps. 50:10 RSV)

Is this writer hedging? He asks: "In a recent column you recommended tithing—that is, giving God ten percent of your income. It's my impression that this is an Old Testament rule, no longer applicable. I think it's optional."

Billy's answer is food for thought.

Of course, how you handle your money is an optional matter. God doesn't force you to distribute it one way or another. There are certain Biblical principles, however, that go to make up a philosophy of Christian stewardship.

For one think, God owns everything. We are custodians, so to speak, of His property (Ps. 50:10). Whatever we give, it is by definition His anyway.

Secondly, one's giving ought to be prompted by love—and by a personal commitment to Christ. That's what Paul explains in II Corinthians 8.

Thirdly, while Christian stewardship is not based on reward, yet it certainly recognizes that there's no better investment in terms of return. Jesus talked in Mark 4 about yields which were thirty-, sixty-, and one-hundred-fold.

The answer to your question about the perpetuation of an Old Testament regulation, however, is simply that if this practice was appropriate under law, it is even more so in this age of freedom and grace. Just check how the Lord amplified the Old Testament regulation on adultery in Matthew 5:28. What would He do with tithing if He discussed it on that basis?

I suspect you are rationalizing for your ungenerous position. Try giving the tithe and more—with joy and even abandon—and you'll see, you'll see!

6

Guilt, Worry, Fear, Loneliness, and Identity

Identity Crisis

Don't let the world around you squeeze you into
its own mold, but let God remold your minds
from within, so that you may prove in practice
that the plan of God for you is good, meets all
his demands and moves toward the goal of true
maturity. (Rom. 12:2 Phillips)

The panorama of Bible characters that all sixty-six
books present shows indeed that none of us has been
endowed with the same set of abilities or liabilities. We
have been created for the same purpose—that of glori-
fying God—yet individuality is the indelible stamp on
each of us.

The problem of identity is a concern the world over.
Politicians and industrialists find it all too easy to gen-
eralize and to lump mankind together in certain classi-
fications, usually for selfish ends. God, however, works
toward maintaining and strengthening personality. Paul
told the Ephesian Christians that in the "body" of
Christ, each "joint" supplies something vital (4:16).
Nobody is to be useless. Nobody is unimportant. Paul
knew from his own experience that he had been personally chosen by Christ and that in the ongoing work
of the church, he had a unique role to play, one which
would eminently utilize his special talents and training
(Acts 22:14).

Keeping a separate identity will be helped by an appraisal of your abilities that pinpoints strength and minimizes weaknesses. Seek the will of God for you individually through prayer and Bible study. Share your experiences whenever possible, and set about some Christian service that suits your schedule and interest.

The identity crisis is ultimately solved when we take the suggestion of Romans 12:1 and present our bodies as a "living sacrifice" to Christ.

The Fellowship of Fear Is Universal

There isn't time for the next generation to solve the problems. They must be solved in this generation or we will perish.

"Terror bombs and incredible guided missiles have carried our world to the brink of destruction." The fellowship of fear is universal. Sir Winston Churchill said we are living in a world balanced by terror. In my talks with President Eisenhower, Churchill, Queen Elizabeth, and other leaders, they have not offered any ultimate hope that we can solve our problems. Economic pressures around the world are exploding North Africa in flames. There are racial flare-ups everywhere. This problem isn't confined to the southern part of the United States. The noose is tightening. History offers us little hope. In 3,000 years we have had 286 years of peace. There isn't time for the next generation to solve the problems. They must be solved in this generation or we perish.

Why Worry?

> Are not five sparrows sold for two pennies? And
> not one of them is forgotten before God. Why,
> even the hairs of your head are all numbered.
> Fear not; you are of more value than many
> sparrows. (Luke 12:6, 7 RSV)

It's never wrong to view life seriously, but if that
means a lot of anxious concern for you, then it is
wrong.

Medical authorities keep telling us of the very real
and very extensive damage that habitual worry can produce. Furthermore, for the Christian it's so unneces-
sary. That's the whole point of Jesus' remarks in Luke
12, where He asks if His hearers have thought of
God's care for the flowers and the birds.

I Feel So Guilty

> Though he slay me, yet will I trust in him. . . .
> (Job 13:15)

*A conscientious woman asks this question: "Is it
wrong to dearly love your family, your new home and
furnishings, and your gardening? Is it wrong to dress
well and teach your children good grooming?"*

Billy Graham's wise answer goes like this:

We've come a long way from the conditions of the
"Plimoth Plantation" about which was written in 1647:
"After their victails were spente . . . they were only to
rest on God's providence; at night not many times
knowing wher to have a bitt of any thing ye next day.
And so, as one well observed, had need to pray that
God would give them ther dayly brade. . . . Yet they
bore these wants with great patience and allacritie of
spirite. . . ."

The contrast between that poverty and our affluence is violent, yet nobody would suggest we go back to such privations. We do need, however, two things: first, the recognition that all the blessings of life come from God (see James 1:17); second, the ability to hold possessions loosely, so that with or without them our basic happiness and ultimate purpose in life are unaffected.

The Book of Job is the story of an affluent man who loved God. Yet when his wealth and even his family were taken away, he still had his integrity and his faith (see 13:15).

Enjoy what things you have and give generously to those in need. But above all, as a Christian, be a good steward-manager, employing everything for the glory of God.

Rationalizing Wrongdoing?

. . . when I want to do right, evil lies close at hand. (Rom. 7:21 RSV)

Here's a realistic question: "I'm surprised lately at how easily I can rationalize wrongdoing. Things I was brought up to reject entirely, now almost seem appealing. And, oh yes, I am a Christian. What can I do to correct this drift?"

Billy's answer is helpful:

We live in an age which dulls the sense of right and wrong. We've been hearing the "gospel" of permissiveness for such a long time that our conscience has almost been persuaded of its merit.

The Bible, however, sets some standards. It says there are some things always right and some things always wrong. But it does more than that. It gives the method whereby we may do right—the wisdom to know what is pleasing to God, and the power to accomplish it. That is all through faith in Christ.

Would you be surprised to know that the great apostle Paul had a problem like yours? You can read of it in Romans 7. He had a tug within him to yield to sin at the same time he had holy inclinations to do right. The resolution of this dilemma was in a total yielding to Jesus Christ, whom, Paul said, always provided victory.

I would think renewed efforts at prayer and Bible reading would help immensely.

Age of Anxiety

> Fear not, therefore; you are of more value than many sparrows. (Matt. 10:31 RSV)

Concern is one thing, but a troubled fear is another. Ever notice the cat or dog sleeping peacefully by the fire? They don't have anxiety. They know they have shelter from the elements; they have food, usually anytime they want it; and they leave the rest to their master.

Human beings, however, are of a higher order. Their capacity for worry is enormous. Sören Kierkegaard, the Danish philosopher, said: "No Grand Inquisitor has in readiness such tortures as has anxiety, and no spy knows how to attack more artfully the man he suspects, choosing the instant when he is the weakest—as anxiety does. It never lets him escape, neither by diversion nor by choice, neither at work nor play, neither by day or night."

Today the pace and problems of life are accelerated. Every generation has more reason for alarm and anxiety than the last. But the supply of peace and confidence that God through faith can provide is sufficient. Read Matthew 10 and you'll understand why in verse 31 Jesus assuringly says, "So don't worry" (LB).

7

Hostility, Temper, Dissatisfaction, and Cynicism

Cynicism Can Throttle Your Hope

I led them with cords of compassion, with the bands of love, and I became to them as one who eases the yoke on their jaws, and I bent down to them and fed them. (Hos. 11:4 RSV)

One of the greatest statements of the love of God is in Hosea 11:8. The prophet quotes God as saying, "How shall I give thee up?" And this was said after an avalanche of rebellion and back sliding.

I think we have to be careful not to attribute to God the feelings so characteristic of men. I agree that if God were human, our conduct, especially in this last decade, would have turned off His love and shut down His saving grace. Fortunately for us, that is not the case.

His love is forever! His mercy endures to the end! That's why the simple gospel of Christ needs to be heard now more than ever. One of the proofs He's still interested is the life-changing conversations I saw last year all over the world.

Don't let cynicism throttle your hope. God is still there, and your sincere invitation to Him to prove it will immediately be honored.

How to Handle Dissatisfactions

> . . . it's a point of maturity to hold lightly the
> affairs of this life and to hold tenaciously the
> bright truths of the world to come.

I'm not saying we should wink at shortcomings. . . .
Our jobs, our salary, our educational system ought to
provide gratifying results, and failing to do that, merit
our attention. But it's a point of maturity to hold
lightly the affairs of this life and to hold tenaciously the
bright truths of the world to come.

People with a prior commitment to Jesus Christ are
the best suited to handle dissatisfactions of all kinds.
They operate on the principle Paul stated in Romans
10:11: ". . . Whosoever believeth on Him shall not be
disappointed." I think the pollsters do us a disservice
by merely repeating the number of those dissatisfied,
and not the reason of those satisfied.

Hostility to God

> To set the mind on the flesh is death, but to
> set the mind on the Spirit is life and peace. For
> the mind that is set on the flesh is hostile to
> God; it does not submit to God's law, indeed it
> cannot; and those who are in the flesh cannot
> please God. (Rom. 8:6-8 RSV)

Opposition to faith is nothing new, and perhaps you
recall that the first question of Satan to those beginning
the human race was one of atheistic doubt (Gen. 3:1).
The mockers have always been with us, but in the secular mood of today their ideas get an increasing audience.

The Bible teaches that by nature we have a bent
toward sin and evil, and that by definition we are op-

posed to God and faith (Rom. 8:7). It is only when the Holy Spirit is permitted, through faith in Christ, to go to work in our minds and hearts that He leads us to truth. He shows us the reality of God, the love of Christ, and the miraculous nature of repentance and faith.

Temper

> He who is slow to anger has great understanding, but he who has a hasty temper exalts folly.
> (Prov. 14:29 RSV)

The Book of Proverbs is known as wisdom literature. The statement in Proverbs 14:19 is particularly appropriate: "He that is slow to wrath is of great understanding: but he that is hasty of spirit exalteth folly."

In the New Testament you have the assertion of Paul that one of the results of Christ's Spirit living within us—through our faith—is self-control. It all really backs up to the issue of a disciplined life. . . . society and custom place certain controls upon us. Maturity teaches us that happy and productive living involves many more than are self-imposed.

. . . Prospective employers shy away from . . . explosive people, and certainly the girls won't relish companionship which a temper can so easily destroy.

Above all . . . being a Christian really means being a little Christ. The same power Jesus knew can . . . conquer . . . any . . . bad habit.

Temper

Be angry but do not·sin; do not let the sun go
down on your anger. (Eph. 4:26 RSV)

*A distressed woman writes Billy Graham: "I lost
control of my temper last night. And I had good reason—I found out my husband had been cheating on
me for months."*

Graham answers this way:

Paul makes an interesting statement to the Ephesian
Christians: "If you are angry, do not let anger lead you
into sin; do not let sunset find you still nursing it. . . ."
(4:26 NEB).

The Bible here does not forbid displeasure, but it
sets up two controls. The first is to keep anger clear of
bitterness, spite, or hatred. The second is to check
daily on whether you have handled malevolent feelings.
There's an old Latin proverb, "He who goes angry to
bed has the devil for a bedfellow."

Of course there are many irritations in life. They become prime opportunities for Satan to lead us into evil
passion. But when aroused by some proper cause and
if under the control of a holy nature, anger can flash
forth with a marvelous power against wickedness, un-
truth, and dishonor.

Jesus was exercised about several things (see Mark
3:5 and John 2:15), but there were no sinful elements
in His divine mind.

My dear lady, it appears you have just cause for
concern. That marital problem of yours must be
handled. Be careful, however, being the Christian you
say you are, that your anger is not without cause, or
without measure, or without justice, and make it always consistent with love.

8

Prayer, Piety,
and Practice

Earnest Prayer

... I will not let thee go, except thou bless me.
(Gen. 32:26)

... I believe it is time for prayer. We talk about
prayer and we preach about it, but how much real
praying do we do? I'm talking about the kind of prayer
that Jacob used when he prayed, "I will not let thee
go, except thou bless me" (Gen. 32:26). Or the prayer
of Moses, "... blot out my name ... from thy
book. ..." (Exod. 32:32 NEB). Or that of Paul, "...
I could wish ... myself accursed ... for the sake of
my brethren. ..." (Rom. 9:3 RSV). Have we done
that kind of praying for America, for our homes, for
our church, for revival?

The Power of Prayer

What power there is in prayer!

What power there is in prayer! I never realized it before in all my young life and ministry. It has given me
a tremendous blessing in my own heart. How would
you feel if you started preaching in a campaign which
had had regular prayer meetings on its behalf for a full
nine months before it started? How would you feel if

every day at noon a prayer meeting was held by scores of people? How would you feel if several all-day prayer meetings had been conducted? How would you react if all-night prayer meetings had been held only a few hundred feet from the place where you were to preach the Word of God? And how would you feel to receive letters, wires, and cablegrams from all parts of the world indicating that the senders were praying for you? . . . It was the people who prayed who made the difference. I can see yet the forty to fifty women who prayed faithfully day after day and then sat in front of the platform with their faces full of expectant faith that God was about to work again that night.

Holy Living

We'll begin to forgive seventy times seven.

. . . your confession means nothing, mine means nothing, unless we repent and turn from that sin. Confession means absolutely nothing to God—He's stopped up His ears. We sin, then we say, "O Lord, I'm sorry I sinned." That's not confession! Confession is repentance of our sins, and turning in yieldedness to Him. . . .

It is time for personal consecration—holy living. When revival comes I believe the members of our churches and our spiritual leaders every day and every moment, in the factory and in the shop and in every place, will begin to live the teachings of the Lord Jesus Christ and the teachings of the New Testament. We'll begin to forgive seventy times seven. We'll begin to turn the other cheek. We'll begin to go the second mile. We'll give our cloak as well as our coat. We'll begin to live by I Corinthians 13, and we'll love one another.

Saying One Thing, Doing Another

> The real source of doubt, in which all lesser doubts seem to be swallowed up, is the apathy and indifference of Christians, saying one thing and doing another.

This is what Graham heard from a sixteen-year-old girl: "My sister, 14, is bugging me about not being a good Christian. How can I convince her I've really changed? Or should I ignore her?"

Billy says this:

Jesus once said, ". . . the way to identify a tree or a person is by the kind of fruit produced" (Matt. 7:20 LB).

While the Christian life depends on qualities that are unseen, it is judged by attitudes and actions that are seen. J. H. Jowett, a great minister of another day, said that the "real source of doubt, in which all lesser doubts seem to be swallowed up, is the apathy and indifference of Christians, saying one thing and doing another." Such then is the importance of demonstrating on the outside what you believe inside.

I certainly would not ignore your sister. That would be neither Christian nor courteous. Why not listen seriously to her complaints? It could be they have some foundation in fact. None of us is beyond correction. If she seems a little harsh, pray for extra love and patience, and let actions, not words, reflect your changed life.

In addition to whatever other Bible reading you may do, read a chapter of Proverbs daily. It's very good in keeping your feet on the ground.

It's Hard to Be a Christian

If God's eagles rise in the storm and His stars shine in the night, you can emerge victorious for your present trial.

A Christian going through trial asks this question: "I know you tell new converts that living the Christian life will not be easy. In my case, it has been terribly hard. Some friends have left me, and often I am the victim of doubts and fears. When will the going get easier?"

Billy's solid and comforting answer is this:

If we are to judge by the statements of the apostle Paul, the going never gets easier (Rom. 7:15-25). But at the same time, the help of God gets greater and the joy of faith stronger.

The sixth chapter of the Book of Acts affords one of Scripture's most dramatic stories. It is of Stephen just prior to his martyrdom. If you feel alone, consider what he experienced when in the council that day—it was Stephen against the world. Probably among all the eyes fastened on him, there was no friendly gaze.

Yet it was at that moment, like the sun breaking through a thunder cloud, that Stephen revealed in his face the splendor of the God who was sustaining him. I don't know why it is that God chooses such moments for this special revelation of Himself, but often it is.

We seem never to know the heights and depths of the spirit world until we are forced into them by circumstance. The spirit touches its pinnacle of triumph often at the very time outward appearances might indicate all is lost.

If God's eagles rise in the storm and His stars shine in the night, you can emerge victorious for your present trial. Keep trusting!

How to Handle Adversity

Great peace have those who love thy law;
nothing can make them stumble. (Ps. 119:165
RSV)

Christians have had to cope with adversity before. In the first century it was persecution. In later times it was theological heresy. In the twentieth century it has been the deadening effect of secularism, plus the disturbing effect of a generation intent on ignoring God.

Practice the presence of Christ daily, and remember that God is still on the throne and at the end will bring order out of chaos. That hope has great comforting effect, and will enable you to say with the Psalmist, "Great peace have they which love thy law: and nothing shall offend them" (119:165).

Coping

The Christian . . . need not despair in the face
of such a dire outlook. He has resources to draw
on which provide stability and hope.

If all the shocking revelations of recent months had come to us in one dose, it might have been almost lethal. In installments, however, we adjust but never quite accept.

The Bible scholar knows that the *end times,* the period before the return of Christ, is not to be known for peace and happiness. It is rather characterized by wars and hate, as the full force of sinful living is revealed (see II Tim. 3).

The Christian, however, need not despair in the face of such a dire outlook. He has resources to draw on which provide stability and hope. When you talk about coping, Paul gives a superb statement in II Corinthians 4. He differentiates between a realistic appraisal of conditions and a supernatural trust which always keeps the ultimate victory of Christ in view.

Work

God has ordained work.

To say that God doesn't like a lazy man is not the whole truth. The Scriptures say that God is love, so He obviously loves everybody. Let's say, however, that a lazy person does not win His commendation. Proverbs 18:9 says, "A lazy man is brother to the saboteur" (LB). Or Paul puts it succinctly when he writes in II Thessalonians 3:10, "He who does not work shall not eat" (LB). The idea of employment may not be too popular with the young, but I've noticed a remarkable change comes over a person between the last year of college and the first year of financial responsibility. God has ordained work. Within certain limits it fills life with satisfaction and purpose.

Our heavenly occupations will be exciting, constructive, and rewarding. The faith that guarantees tomorrow has to be a reality today. I hope you have it.

Winning Daily Victories over Temptation and Sin

". . . I will put my spirit within you, and cause you to walk in my statutes. . . . (Ezek. 36:27 RSV)

. . . because the Spirit resides in you, you now have the prospect of winning daily victories over temptation and sin. "There hath no temptation taken you but such as is common to man: but God is faithful, who will not suffer you to be tempted above that ye are able; but will with the temptation also make a way to escape, that ye may be able to bear it" (I Cor. 10:13). The Bible teaches that you are now to "abhor that which is evil" (Rom. 12:9) and "put . . . on the Lord Jesus Christ, and make not provision for the flesh, to fulfill the lusts thereof" (13:14).

But how can you do this? Where do you get such a capacity and such strength? God once said through Ezekiel the prophet, ". . . I will put my spirit within you, and cause you to walk in my statutes. . . ." (Ezek. 36:27). Your victory will come from the Spirit of God within you, never as a result of your own struggles. You need only to believe in and yield to Him to receive His help in resisting sin. Through faith you can become "more than conquerors" (Rom. 8:37).

To the Cross with Him

> Then Jesus told his disciples, "If any man would come after me, let him deny himself and take up his cross and follow me." (Matt. 16:24 RSV)

. . . the cross of Christ is an offense because it sets forth an imperative ideal of life. Jesus said, "If any man will come after me, let him deny himself, and take up his cross, and follow me" (Matt. 16:24). We are busy in our churches today building astronomical figures, sending in reports of how many new members we took in and how many people affiliated with the church. Jesus worked on the opposite end. Every time the crowd got too big, Jesus would say, "All right, deny yourself if you want to follow me." That eliminated about half of them. To those remaining He would say, "All right, if you are going to follow me, take up the cross." That eliminated almost all the rest of them. They did not want self-denial; they wanted a kingdom, they wanted a crown, they wanted to rule, to live in a palace. They wanted all the blessings of the Christian life, but they were not going to go to the cross with Him. How many chafe at the restraint of a life like Christ's! We refuse to give up what we know His cross condemns.

The Joy of God on Their Faces

There was a strange warmness that filled my heart to overflowing.

Billy Graham visited Dohnavur in India to see the orphanage founded by Amy Carmichael. As he surveyed the orphans, he exclaimed, "Just look at them. They have the joy of God on their faces. There seems to be more concentrated happiness here than any place I have ever seen."

I had something very strange and unusual happen to me at Dohnavur. I cannot yet quite explain it, but I know it must have been from God. As I walked around the grounds, I could not keep back the tears—in fact, I could hardly talk. There was a strange warmness that filled my heart to overflowing.

I went in to see a Miss Waite, who was Miss Carmichael's nurse for so many years. Tomorrow is her eighty-second birthday. As I was talking to her, I broke down and started crying. I had to turn away. Then I said, "Let's pray." Just as I started to pray, I started weeping. I prayed, "Oh, God, I feel as if we are on holy ground." I asked John Bolten to pray, and he wept and prayed. I could not even say goodby to Miss Waite. I was so filled with a strange emotion and I could not account for it.

We walked about the place, seeing the children and young people. Then we had lunch with some of the workers. We went to Miss Carmichael's room. There we saw the print of where her bed had sat for so many years; twenty years she had been an invalid before she died; twenty years her body was wracked with pain.

All around the bed were pictures of mountains. They said she loved mountains because she was always on the mountain top.

They said she had the faculty of making everyone who came into her presence feel as though he or she were the only person in the world. They said she ran Dohnavur from her bedside, kept complete control of it, and yet had the wonderful ability of delegating authority.

A Formula to Regulate Attitude and Actions

I test a proposition by asking four questions. . . .

For years I have used a simple formula, which stems from reading of Scripture, to regulate my attitude and actions. I test a proposition by asking four questions:

1. Is the attitude or action to the glory of God?
2. Can I ask God's blessing on it?
3. Is it a stumbling block to myself or others?
4. Does it contribute to a healthy, moral atmosphere?

Wheat and Tares

> . . . in the time of harvest I will say to the
> reapers, Gather ye together first the tares, and
> bind them in bundles to burn them; but gather
> the wheat into my barn. (Matt. 13:30)

. . . we have seen a strange paradox that often con-
fused and bewildered me. We have seen a revival of religious interest throughout the United States but an ac-
celeration of crime, divorce, and immorality. Within
the church there is a new depth of commitment, a new
sense of destiny, and a spirit of revival, yet in the
world there is an intensification of the forces of evil.
Crime is on the increase. Fear haunts the council halls
of the nations. Wars, hot and cold, are being spawned
across the world. Family life is threatened by evil
forces. And in many places there is a stark lack of social concern. The tares of evil flourish even in the same
field with the growing grain of righteousness. But we
forget that Christ said: ". . . in the time of harvest I
will say to the reapers, Gather ye together first the
tares, and bind them in bundles to burn them: but
gather the wheat into my barn" (Matt. 13:30). The
wheat and the tares are destined to grow side by side;
when wheat is sown, the Devil sows tares. But a day of
separation, an ultimate triumph for truth and righteousness, is coming.

Risen!

He is not here: for he is risen, as he said. . . .
(Matt. 28:6)

On Sunday morning, as the sun was rising on the eastern horizon and the light was filling all the cracks and crevices where the darkness had been a few moments ago, Mary and Mary Magdalene came sorrowfully with tears streaming down their cheeks. Their Lord and their Master was dead! They intended to anoint His body with perfume and spices. When they got to the tomb, they saw that something was wrong and then they were more afraid than before. The stone had been rolled away and they saw a man standing there. He was different from any man they had ever seen. Scripture says that his clothes were like lightning. Did you ever see lightning flash? Just hold the flash of lightning and you will see what the man looked like that day. He was as brilliant as the noon-day sun, and the women trembled and were afraid. This shining one said, "Be not afraid," and then he gave the greatest message that has ever been heard by any human ear. There has never been a message comparable to the message that day, two thousand years ago, at the tomb of Jesus Christ: "He is not here: for he is risen, as he said. . . ."

All of Hell Laughed

The people gathered about the cross, laughing and scoffing.

So they took Jesus away. They put a crown of thorns upon His brow; they put spikes in His hands and feet. Then they raised Him on a cross to crucify Him between heaven and earth.

One of the malefactors on the right hand turned to Him and said, "Lord, remember me when thou comest into thy kingdom."

Jesus replied, "Today shalt thou be with me in paradise." The people gathered about the cross, laughing and scoffing. " 'Today shalt thou be with me in paradise'—what does He say?"

Finally He cried out, "It is finished." Then all of hell laughed, saying, " Boy, we have got Him now. He claimed to be the Son of God, but now He is dead, He is finished, and He himself admits that he is finished."

A great artist painted a picture of the crucifixion of Jesus Christ. On the bottom of it he wrote "Finished." Someone came along later and erased it and said, "Sir, we are going to put the word *beginning* instead of *finished* because redemption was finished, but life was begun in Jesus Christ."

Let This Cup Pass

. . . O My Father, if it be possible, let this cup pass from me. . . . (Matt. 26:39)

Then you remember that after this they went into the Garden of Gethsemane, and there the Lord Jesus began to pray. As He prayed, He said, "O Lord, if it be possible, let this cup pass from Me. O Father, if there is any other way to redeem the world, if there is any other way of salvation, if you can do it any other way, Lord, do it." But in the providence of God and to fulfill the Word of God, the Lord Jesus was slain. He gave Himself because He loved you and me. There at Gethsemane the Lord Jesus said, "Nevertheless, not My will but Thine be done." The Lord Jesus was willing to endure suffering, was willing to have God turn His back, was willing to die because He loved us and did not want us to spend eternity in hell.

The Purpose of the "Silent Years"

. . . the child grew and became strong, filled with wisdom; and the favor of God was upon him. . . . and Jesus increased in wisdom and in stature, and in favor with God and man. (Luke 2:40, 52 RSV)

The "silent years," as they are called, extend from Christ's return to Nazareth as an infant to His baptism by John as an adult. The only exception to this silence is an incident in which Jesus, Mary, and Joseph went to Jerusalem and the temple in his twelfth year.

May I suggest that these "unreported" years served a worthwhile purpose—something in fact we have forgotten about today. That is a time of quiet development and a gaining of experience. Christ needed it before He went to the cross as the Savior of the world.

The Bible says that during this time Jesus "became a strong robust lad" and "grew both tall and wise ... loved by God and man" (Luke 2:40, 52 LB).

You see, the incarnation, that is, God's Son in the flesh, was a true acceptance of humanity. His schooling was probably that of an ordinary child. He worked at

Joseph's carpenter's bench. But above all, His mind was nourished on the Scriptures and spiritual things.

Wouldn't you agree with me that in our busy society where everything requires gratification, we need such a quiet time? A quiet time when we can nourish our souls, commune with God—and prepare for communication with men. Without it we will never make it through the turbulent days ahead.

The Deity of Christ

> If we receive the testimony of men, the testimony of God is greater; for this is the testimony of God that he has borne witness to his Son. He who believes in the Son of God has the testimony in himself. He who does not believe God has made him a liar. . . . (I John 5:9, 10 RSV)

Can a person be a Christian and reject the deity of Christ? Absolutely not! It is a contradiction in terms, and the Bible gives a clear answer: ". . . God declares that Jesus is his Son. All who believe this know in their hearts that it is true. If anyone doesn't believe this, he is actually calling God a liar . . ." (I John 5:9, 10 LB).

I thank God for higher education and for the varied kinds of theological training available today. We need, however, always to guard against theoretical and philosophical gymnastics which exalt human speculation and minimize divine revelation.

If Christ isn't deity, then the gospel has made a mockery of us all. I can tell you, however, on the basis of changed lives which I have observed around the world, He is God, all right, and He is willing to prove it in every believing heart.

Obey Christ

Christ is the head of the church and He has
commanded you to worship and serve Him
there.

. . . obey Christ. You must live for Christ. I have
searched the Bible from cover to cover and no place
can I find where it says you can be a Christian and live
any kind of life you want to live. How do you obey
Christ? You obey Christ by reading your Bible every
day. The Bible is food for your soul. It helps you to
grow. You obey Christ by spending time in prayer every day. You can pray anywhere—walking down the
street, sitting in your home, or driving your car. God
will hear your prayers and answer them. You obey
Christ by witnessing for Him. How do you witness?
You witness, first of all, by the way you live. People
will see you are different and begin to ask questions.
Then tell them about Christ. Another way you obey
Christ is by being faithful in your church. Christ is the
head of the church and He has commanded you to
worship and serve Him there.

East and West

I like to picture Christ as one who can stretch
out His arms to the East and West.

There are some people in the Far East who have the
idea that Christianity is a Western religion. That is not
true. Christianity was in the East long before it was in
the West. Christ was born between the East and
the West. His skin was not as light as mine nor was it
as dark as that of some of the people who live in the

East. I like to picture Christ as one who can stretch out His arms to the East and West.

Heaven's Best and Earth's Best

> . . . God has highly exalted him and bestowed on him the name which is above every name. (Phil. 2:9 RSV)

I do not recall ever trying to make Christ a superman or circus strong man. But while He was gentle, quiet, and meek, He was also a militant leader whose influence and teaching took the shackles off the slaves, lifted woman to a new position, and shook the foundations of the Roman Empire, and whose influence has caused the fall of dictators even up to the present. I have often said that Jesus Christ was a composite man, made up of heaven's best and earth's best, and that I do not think He was like the effeminate, emaciated conceptions of some artists.

The Cross and the Resurrection

> More and more I try to put the cross at the center of my message. . . . Somehow we must recapture the thrilling realization that Jesus lives and that he who believes in Him, "though he were dead, yet shall he live. . . ."

My faith in the centrality of the cross has also deepened. Christ said " . . . I, when I am lifted up from the earth, will draw all men to myself" (John 12:32 RSV). The cross reveals the sins of men, and it also reveals the unwearying love of God. There is power in the pronouncement that Christ died for our sins "according to the Scriptures." More and more I try to put the cross at the center of my message, and I find that when I fail to do this something is lacking in my presentation. The great apostle Paul declared, ". . . I decided to know nothing among you except Jesus Christ and him crucified" (I Cor. 2:2 RSV).

The years have also deepened my conviction that the resurrection of Christ needs to be proclaimed with greater emphasis. Most of us proclaim it only at Easter time, but the New Testament breathes the spirit of the resurrection throughout. It was the fact of an empty tomb that drove the early disciples to turn the world upside down. Somehow we must recapture the thrilling realization that Jesus lives and that he who believes in Him, "though he were dead, yet shall he live" (John 11:25).

10

Salvation

What Is the "Heart"?

> . . . man believes with his heart and so is justified, and he confesses with his lips and so is saved. (Rom. 10:10 RSV)

As the central organ in the body, representing a focus of vital action, the heart has come to stand for all moral, intellectual, and spiritual life. As one has defined it, "the heart is the place in which the process of self-consciousness is carried out, in which the soul is at home with itself." So many popular songs use the word *heart* to mean the seat of the emotions.

Thus the Old Testament commands that you "know . . . your heart" (Deut. 8:5 RSV) and later laments the fact that "none considereth in his heart" (Isa. 44:19).

The Bible teaches the radical corruption of human nature and relates this to the heart. Exodus 8:15 says the heart can be "hardened," and Jeremiah 17:9 says that the heart is "deceitful . . . and desperately wicked."

The good news of the gospel, however, is that if we let Him, God can change out hearts. As the place where God's law is written (Rom. 2:15), it can also become the arena for a work of God's grace (Acts 15:9). Paul in Romans says that it is with the heart that we believe unto eternal life (10:10).

Whatever term you use to represent that which is innermost and deepest and most important, it is just at that place where God meets us in a personal faith.

Is the Judgment Day Coming?

> . . . on that day . . . God judges the secrets of men by Christ Jesus. (Rom. 2:16 RSV)

In an age of constant and far-reaching change, few things remain sure. But this is certain, that a time of judgment and retribution awaits our race in the future.

Several things suggest it. First, the administration of moral government in this world requires it. The way good and evil is presently distributed, the incidence of prosperity and adversity among men is seldom in harmony with their respective characters. For example, Paul is in prison while the mad Nero is on the throne.

Secondly, I think conscience anticipates the coming of such a day. The voice within testifies to the solemn truth that after death comes judgment.

Thirdly and most importantly, the Bible declares the arrival of such an event. See statements like Matthew 12:36, Acts 17:31, Romans 2:16, and Jude 14, 15.

But now, the whole thrust of the gospel is that we don't need to fear such a day. Wrote John in I John 4:17: "Herein is our love made perfect, that we may have boldness in the day of judgment. . . ." Thank God that what Christ has done will make us acceptable to the Father, and we need not fear condemnation at the divine bar.

Mental Illness and Conversion

A key word . . . is *realities.*

While it is true that some mental illnesses take on a religious aspect, to link the two as cause and effect would be as unfounded as claiming that because a cat likes the warmth of a fire, she could ignite one of her own.

It may well be that some emotional upset sets the stage for a surrender to God. I assure you, however, that the new life of the Spirit is a miracle, not a malady. The Scripture presents Jesus as the Physician (Luke 5:31, 32) who heals the sick soul.

Christian conversion is a phenomenon which has been well-documented by such eminent psychologists as William James and Carl Jung.

In his study *Varieties of Religious Experience,* William James says: "To be converted, to be regenerated, to receive grace, to experience religion, to gain assurance, are so many phrases which denote the process, gradual or sudden, by which a self hitherto divided, and consciously wrong, inferior and unhappy, becomes unified and consciously right, superior and happy, in consequence of its firmer hold on religious realities" (p. 186). A key word there is *realities.*

I believe so strongly in the power of Christian conversion to change lives for the better that I have devoted my life to that task.

God is careful to assure us that "his Holy Spirit speaks to us . . . and tells us that we really are God's children. . . ." (Rom. 8:16 LB). No book, psychiatrist, or inner doubt can stand up against that.

God Is at Work

Never have so many people been so open to
the gospel.

God is at work in a remarkable way. Never have so
many people been so open to the gospel. In parts of
Asia, there are evidences of the outpouring of God's
Spirit in evangelism. In Korea the churches are increasing four times faster than the population. In certain
parts of northeast India, Christians now form a major-
ity of the population and are bringing about a whole
new dimension of civic righteousness. In Papua, New
Guinea, a land where the gospel was virtually unknown
before this generation, a large percentage of the people
now profess faith in Christ. Latin Americans are re-
sponding to the gospel in unprecedented numbers, and
evangelical churches in many parts of Latin America
are multiplying vigorously. . . .

In 1945 Christians in Africa numbered about twenty
million. Today they number at least seventy million.
Africa, south of the Sahara, could become substantially
Christian by the end of the century, in spite of many
dangers, obstacles, and even persecutions in some ar-
eas.

The Wrath to Come

If I believed the way you believe, I would crawl
across England on broken blass to warn people.

Notice the terms Jesus uses to describe the state of
the lost: "a place of wailing," "a place of weeping," "a

furnace of fire," "a place of torment," "a place of outer darkness," "a place of everlasting punishment," "a place prepared for the devil and his angels." Our Lord further said, "He that believeth on the Son hath everlasting life: and he that believeth not the Son shall not see life; but the wrath of God abideth on him" (John 3:36).

Many years ago, a man in England on his way to the gallows was being warned by the Anglican chaplain of the "wrath to come" unless he repented. He turned to the chaplain and said, "If I believed the way you believe, I would crawl across England on broken glass to warn people."

The Gospel Is . . .

. . . in grateful obedience I should live a life "rich in good works."

The gospel is an announcement of the good news. But what good news? It is the thrilling proclamation that Jesus Christ, very God and very man, died for my sins on the cross, was buried, and rose the third day. The Son has made full atonement for my sins. If I reach forth by faith to receive Christ as my personal Savior, I am declared forgiven by God, not through any merit of mine but through the merits of Christ's shed blood. I rejoice in pardon for the past, the indwelling presence of the Holy Spirit for the present, and the living hope for the future. The great philosophical questions concerning where I came from, why I am here, and where I am going are answered, and in grateful obedience I should live a life "rich in good works."

Businessmen Ask a Question

> . . . when a man makes a choice, he improves
> or degrades his world.

Over and over, businessmen tell me, "I want to turn
to God, but how do I do it?" May I answer that right
here, even though doing so in a secular magazine may
appear to be unusual?

First, recognize that God so loved you that he gave
His Son to die on the cross. Second, repent, turning
your back on sin. Third, surrender yourself, receiving
Jesus Christ as your Savior and Lord, and asking His
guidance. That's it—the beginning of a relationship
that might change this world.

Some moralists allege that our Bible is not relevant to
modern business problems. True, the Bible doesn't go
into capital investment, automation, or conglomeration.
True, its commands only prescribe relationships between God and man, and between man and his fellows.
True, the Biblical economy was agrarian and not in-
dustrial.

But consider this: no business practice in modern
life exists except because of the relationships between
men. So the old law is relevant.

In modern business nothing is left to chance. Nor in
government. President Eisenhower once said, "This
history of free men is never really written by chance
but by choice—their choice." And when a man makes
a choice, he improves or degrades his world.

This Hour of Crisis

> If you become Christ's man, you will stumble
> upon wonder after wonder, and every wonder
> will be true.

What a moment to be an ambassador for Christ;
what an hour for the proclamation of His gospel!
Christianity is the religion of crisis. For a world in fer-
ment it is made to order, for it fits the heart and needs
of man like a glove. This is the time to make Christ
known, whether we be pastor, teacher, evangelist, or
layman. I intend by the grace of God to continue in my
ordained calling until He says, "It is enough."

I recall a magnificent saying of Brindon to King
Brude, uttered long ago. "What shall I find if I accept
your gospel and become Christ's man?" asked the king.
Brindon replied, "If you become Christ's man, you will
stumble upon wonder after wonder, and every wonder
will be true." If in this hour of crisis we will dare to be
Christ's men, even in a time of blighting disillusion-
ment, we will come upon wonder after wonder, and every wonder will be true.

The Hero and Idol of My Heart

> . . . in thy presence is fulness of joy; at thy
> right hand there are pleasures for evermore. (Ps.
> 16:11)

When the invitation was given, I made my way to
the front with the others. I gave my hand to the
preacher (Mordecai Ham) and my heart to the Savior.
Immediately joy, peace, and assurance flooded my
soul. My sins, which were many, were gone! For the

first time I had met the person who became the Hero of my life.

I had sought thrills! I found them in Christ. I had looked for something that would bring perfect joy and happiness! I found it in Christ. I had looked for something that would bring pleasure and that would satisfy the deepest longing of my heart! I found it in Christ. "... in thy presence is fulness of joy; at thy right hand there are pleasures for evermore" (Ps. 16:11).

Christ is the Hero and Idol of my heart. He challenges, thrills, and satisfies.

What Can I Do with My Load of Sin?

As far as the east is from the west, so far does he remove our transgressions from us. (Ps. 103:12 RSV)

Do you remember the train load of poison gas that became a national issue? It was in danger of leaking, and the big question was: Where could it be safely deposited? Finally they hauled it out into the Atlantic and sank it. Each of us carries a load of sin more poisonous than any gas. We ignore it as long as we can, but eventually it begins to leak. We try to drown our awareness of it with drugs, alcohol, or frenzied activity. We try to unload it on friends, clergymen, or psychiatrists. There is only one safe depository—it is at the cross of Jesus Christ, the only place where sins can be totally blotted out without poisoning others.

Salvation and Our Emotions

If we are faithless he remains faithful—for he cannot deny himself. (II Tim. 2:13 RSV)

When you talk about the emotional side effects of confessing faith in Christ, or being "saved," the Scripture indicates the whole gamut of reaction.

In Acts 16, for example, you have a jailer converted in an emotional outburst that Paul had to stop. In the same chapter, however, you have the conversion of a business woman named Lydia. As far as we can tell, she entered the kingdom quietly and unemotionally. Now there are both ends of the emotional spectrum.

Personal salvation is a transaction brought about by God's Holy Spirit and made possible by an overt act of the will, through repentance and faith. It is the acceptance of and commitment to Jesus Christ as Savior and Lord. The emotions are activated as a side effect of the step of faith, and I suppose vary considerably from person to person.

I suggest you be sure your salvation is grounded on the principles of the Bible and not on an exhilarating and isolated ... encounter. The glow may come and go, but the new life in Jesus is a constant reality (see II Tim. 2:13).

All Have Sinned

... all have sinned, and come short of the glory of God. (Rom. 3:23)

You have a problem tonight of sin. You say, "I'm not troubled with sin." Then you are the only one in the world outside of Christ who is not troubled with sin, because the Bible says, ". . . all have sinned, and come short of the glory of God" (Rom. 3:23). The Bible says, ". . . the wages of sin is death. . . ." (Rom. 6:23) and ". . . the soul that sinneth, it shall die" (Ezek. 18:4). The Bible says, ". . . in sin did my mother conceive me." I was born in sin, and I have the problem of sin to deal with and to face, and the only One who has the answer is the Lord Jesus Christ on the cross of Calvary. There is no answer aside from Him. There is no way of cleansing from sin outside of Christ. "There is none other name under heaven, given among men, whereby we must be saved." The Lord Jesus Christ is the only way!

Confession of Sin

If a man walks in on Sunday morning in his work clothes, he will be probably be turned out.

. . . it is time for confession of sin. We must say as Isaiah said, "Woe is me! . . . I am a man of unclean lips, and I dwell in the midst of a people of unclean lips. . . ." (6:5).

We are guilty of pride. How the devil slips this keen-edged sword into our lives. But not a mention is made in the Word that we are to pray for humility. The Scripture says that we are to humble ourselves—that's our job.

We are guilty of division. We are guilty of worldliness. We are guilty of the commercialism we have in evangelical circles today! Let's confess it; let's face ourselves for a moment. De Quincey once said, "Salute thyself, and see what thy soul doth wear." Let's salute ourselves, let's look in the mirror for a moment, and admit we're guilty of commercialism.

We are guilty of class and color distinction. Dr. So-and-so has the swanky church; he's got "the better people" in his church. If a man walks in on Sunday morning in his work clothes, he will probably be turned out. The church is on the tail end—to our shame!—of progress along racial lines in America today. The church should be leading instead of following.

We are guilty of spiritual lethargy. Sometimes we sit about like overstuffed toads, and we croak and grunt at the right place with a sleepy "Amen" and a weak "Hallelujah."

The Origin of Prophecy

> . . . no prophecy of scripture is a matter of
> one's own interpretation, because no prophecy
> ever came by the impulse of man, but men
> moved by the Holy Spirit spoke from God. (II
> Peter 1:20, 21 RSV)

In the King James Version it reads, ". . . no
prophecy is of any private interpretation. . . ." (II Peter 1:20). Perhaps the meaning is better expressed, "of
no private origination."

What Peter is declaring is that the statements of the
Bible regarding the future are never something of the
prophet's own doing. It is not man's conjecture about
future events. Peter further adds: ". . . no prophecy
ever came by the will of man, but men spoke from
God, being moved by the Holy Spirit."

The marvelous thing about the Scripture is that it is
indeed God speaking to the human heart and to the
soul needs of mankind. We need never doubt its
message. And there's an extra bonus! The Lord has
provided that the same Holy Spirit who helped guide
the writers' pens comes to give understanding and clar-
ity to every reader.

None of this is a put-down for the pastors, teachers,
and preachers who regularly "interpret" Scripture.
Theirs is a God-given task. But it does say that a person without the benefit of anyone or anything else can
find the true salvation.

The Bible Is the Word of God

> Belief exhilarates the human spirit; doubt depresses. Nothing is gained psychologically or spiritually by casting aspersions on the Bible.

Even a casual study of church history will reveal that the great giants of pulpit and pen, from Augustine to Wesley, relied heavily on Scripture for their authority. In this they followed a sacred precedent hallowed by Christ and the apostles.

In 1949 I had been having a great many doubts concerning the Bible. I thought I saw apparent contradictions in Scripture. Some things I could not reconcile with my restricted concept of God. When I stood up to preach, the authoritative note so characteristic of all great preachers of the past was lacking. Like hundreds of other young seminary students, I was waging the intellectual battle of my life. The outcome could certainly affect my future ministry.

In August of that year I had been invited to Forest Home, Presbyterian conference center high in the mountains outside Los Angeles. I remember walking down a trail, tramping into the woods, and almost wrestling with God. I dueled with my doubts, and my soul seemed to be caught in the crossfire. Finally, in desperation, I surrendered my will to the living God revealed in Scripture. I knelt before the open Bible and said: "Lord, many things in this Book I do not understand. But Thou hast said, 'The just shall live by faith.' All I have received from Thee, I have taken by faith. Here and now, by faith, I accept the Bible as Thy Word. I take it all. I take it without reservations. Where there are things I cannot understand, I will reserve judgment until I receive more light. If this pleases Thee, give me authority as I proclaim Thy Word, and through that authority convict me of sin and turn sinners to the Savior."

The Bible's Authority Creates Faith

> . . . the word of God is quick, and powerful,
> and sharper than any twoedged sword. . . . (Heb.
> 4:12)

During the Los Angeles crusade I discovered the secret that changed my ministry. I stopped trying to prove that the Bible was true. I had settled in my own mind that it was, and this faith was conveyed to the audience. Over and over again I found myself saying, "The Bible says . . ." I felt as though I were merely a voice through which the Holy Spirit was speaking.

Authority created faith. Faith generated response, and hundreds of people were impelled to come to Christ. A crusade scheduled for three weeks lengthened into eight weeks, with hundreds of thousands of people in attendance. The people were not coming to hear great oratory, nor were they interested merely in my ideas. I found they were desperately hungry to hear what God had to say through His holy Word.

I felt as though I had a rapier in my hand and, through the power of the Bible, was slashing deeply into men's consciences, leading them to surrender to God. Does not the Bible say of itself, "For the word of God is quick, and powerful, and sharper than any twoedged sword, piercing even to the dividing asunder of soul and spirit, and of the joints and marrow, and is a discerner of the thoughts and intents of the heart" (Heb. 4:12)

I found that the Bible became a flame in my hands. That flame melted away unbelief in the hearts of the people and moved them to decide for Christ. The

Word became a hammer breaking up stony hearts and shaping them into the likeness of God.

When the Sun Shines on the Bible

> Thy word is a lamp to my feet and a light to my path. (Ps. 119:105 RSV)

It was an old English clergyman who suggested an apt comparison between the Bible and a sundial. He said that a person could well read the figures on a dial, but would obviously know nothing of the exact hour unless the sun was shining upon it. Similarly, he suggested, a person could read the Bible through, but unless the Spirit of God was permitted to enlighten the Word it was just a compilation of lofty but abstract ideas.

Christ, Surrender, and the Bible

> "You search the scriptures, because you think that in them you have eternal life; and it is they that bear witness to me." (John 5:39 RSV)

You surrender your life to Christ, through personal repentance and faith, and then watch the ways in which all spiritual input is enhanced—church attendance, fellowship with other Christians, and Bible reading.

The value of Bible reading is not in some magical return on time invested—like four blessings for every two chapters. Jesus said in John 5:39 to search the Scriptures for "they are they which testify of me." When the Bible serves, then, as an introduction to the person of Christ, it is fulfilling God's original design.

The Bible and Heaven

I bless the Lord who gives me counsel. . . .
(Ps. 16:7 RSV)

It's very commendable to want to get back to original languages, but you would need to be a linguist to understand the language form of ancient people.

Nobody has an original Bible, or what is called an "autograph copy." These documents disappeared or were destroyed centuries ago. We can thank God, however, that what we do have comes pretty close and makes no alteration in the original meaning. Evangelical Christians believe the Bible was divinely inspired in the initial writing. They also believe that God's Spirit has superintended even the transmission of Scripture through the years, so that doctrinal errors were avoided.

In any analytical approach to the Bible, however, just remember this: the Scripture was given not to tell how the heavens go, but, through faith in Christ, how to go to heaven. That it does beautifully, simply, and effectively.

The Power of the Word of God

People, I found, cannot stand under the impact of the Word of God.

How foolish I have been so many times. I have worked so hard to build a message, replete with illustrations, with perhaps an experience or two of my own thrown in. True, God blessed those messages in the past. But, oh, how He blessed the plain and simple

Word of God in this campaign! "The Scriptures say.... The Bible says.... The Scriptures say.... The Bible says...." I got to the place where I couldn't preach any of the old sermons. Studying from six to eight hours a day, I received new sermons, burned into my heart by God. I did away with all illustrations. I used from twenty-five to one hundred passages of Scripture each evening. People, I found, cannot stand under the impact of the Word of God. Even the hardest sinner will capitulate.

12

God's Love,
Care, and Holiness

The Holiness of God

... God is not in the winking business.

... it is time for a renewed emphasis on the holiness of God. Every great revival that ever came in the history of the world, or in the history of the church, laid great emphasis on the holiness of God. Study the nature of God. Get every Scripture that you can find on the holiness and righteousness and purity of God, and study it and breathe it on your knees, and you will be a different man or a different woman. Study it, breathe it, digest it, read it—until it grips your soul. God is a holy God.

We think that somehow or other God is going to work some special dispensation for us because we are "fundamental" and because we are "orthodox" in doctrine. We feel that because we have a corner on truth, God has a special dispensation for all of us, and we can go out and gossip and be filled with pride and worldliness and all the rest, and God will overlook it and wink at it. But God is not in the winking business. God holds us responsible for our sins, and the reason we are doing no more than we are today is because of our inward sins. It must cut the very heart of our Christ.

84

The Atomic Power of God

We don't have to live lives of defeat.

His resurrection means that there is power for a victorious life. Paul prayed that the Ephesians might know "what is the exceeding greatness of his power to usward who believe, according to the working of his mighty power, which he wrought in Christ, when he raised him from the dead...." (1:19, 20). Scripture says that the same power, the same energy, the same atomic power God used to raise Christ from the dead is the power that He gives me to live victoriously every day. Isn't that wonderful? We don't have to live lives of defeat. I don't have to go around with a long face, but I can go around with a smile, with my shoulders back, realizing that I have been washed by the blood of Jesus Christ and adopted into the family of God and that now I am His son. I'm a member of the royal family of heaven by adoption into God's family. The same power that raised Christ from the dead gives me power to have daily victory over sin. Isn't that wonderful? The people who have peace in their lives are the people who know Jesus Christ. The only people who are truly happy in the world are the people who know Christ.

Does God Know About Our Loss?

> . . . as the heavens are high above the earth, so
> great in his steadfast love toward those who fear
> him. . . . As a father pities his children, so the
> Lord pities those who fear him. For he knows
> our frame; he remembers that we are dust. (Ps.
> 103:11, 13, 14 RSV)

*An elderly woman writes this: "Right before my
eyes, our pet beagle was run over by a truck. My husband and I are elderly, and this dog meant so much to
us. My question is: Does God know about our loss,
and will we ever see the dog again?"*

Billy shares his views:

First, on the matter of God understanding events
here on earth, according to Matthew 10:29 He certainly knew of your pet's sudden death. Jesus said that
not one sparrow can fall to the ground without your
Father knowing it. Then about your own feelings: consider the Psalmist's statement, "He is like a father to
us, tender and sympathetic. . . ." (103:13 LB). The
Hebrews writer also says that God "understands our
weaknesses" (4:15 LB).

Then regarding the suggestion about seeing the dog
again, the Bible does not indicate this possibility. Only
man has a soul which is eternal and which survives
physical death. This is what distinguishes man from the
brute creation.

It's of interest in the doubling of Job's possessions in
Job 42 that his children were exceptions. That was to
be expected. Since the first ten children were still ex-
isting in the spirit state, he thus needed only seven
more sons and three more daughters.

Your pet is gone, yet God is near. His tender conso-
lations will sustain you.

God's Care

". . . do not be anxious about your life, what
you shall eat or what you shall drink, nor about
your body, what you shall put on. Is not life
more than food, and the body more than cloth-
ing? Look at the birds of the air: they neither
sow nor reap nor gather into barns, and yet your
heavenly Father feeds them. Are you not of
more value than they?" (Matt. 6:25, 26 RSV)

There's a Swedish gospel song that has the following
words: "The care of His child and treasure is a charge
that on Himself He laid." It refers to the self-assigned
task Christ has of watching over His followers. And if
the Savior is thus monitoring our well-being, what can
our worry add to that?

We should be serious about life to the extent we use
caution and common sense, making all due preparation
for our welfare and future. But beyond that lies the
quiet assurance that God superintends the affairs of life
and that in His beneficent plan He does all things well.

The Last First?

. . . while we serve God out of gratitude and
not for compensation, yet He can be trusted finally for a surprising and unmerited reward.

Jesus said, "So the last will be first, and the first
last" (Matt. 20:16 RSV). That statement, and the
whole parable of the laborers which precedes it, has always been difficult to interpret. The secret, however, is
to connect it to the earlier story of the rich young man
and also to the question of Peter.

You see, Peter seemed to imagine that because he
had sacrificed for Christ, the Master was bound to give
him a reward. To be sure, Jesus did promise a reward,

but He wanted here to rebuke that attitude which motivates service merely for the sake of remuneration.

The story of the laborers, some of whom came at different times but all of whom got the same pay, revealed a commercial spirit of bargaining and jealousy. Jesus showed them that all who work in His service will receive all they deserve, but that there will be surprises. The amazement will come not because any receive so little, but that some will receive so much.

There's a tremendous truth here. God, who is sovereign in bestowing His rewards, understands that some have little opportunity for their service and that their ability is limited, but He proves to them the liberality of His loving heart.

Summing up, then, here's the lesson: while we serve God out of gratitude and not for compensation, yet He can be trusted finally for a surprising and unmerited reward.

God Loves You

> . . . God so loved the world, that he gave his only begotten Son, that whosoever believeth in him should not perish, but have everlasting life. (John 3:16)

God loves you. He cares for you. He knows everything about you. Don't ever think this is such a great big world that God doesn't have time for you. He has the hairs of your head counted and He has a name for every hair. He knows where you live. He knows every thought of your head and heart.

I was walking along one day and accidentally stepped on an ant hill. Many of the ants were killed. Scores were hurt. Their home was wrecked. I felt very sorry for the ants. I wanted to tell them how sorry I was and help them rebuild their home, but I couldn't do it. I was too big and they were too little. We couldn't talk to each other.

God looked down from heaven one day. He saw all the unhappiness and trouble in the world. He loves us and wanted to help us. But He was too big and we were too little. We couldn't understand. What did God do? He did the most astounding thing ever done. God decided to become a man. That man was Jesus Christ. Jesus Christ is God. He walked among us. He spoke our language. He healed the sick. He made the blind to see, the deaf to hear, and the lame to walk. He was God.

13

The Church

Out of Grief and Tragedy, a Heroic Church

We learned that the secret of their strength is their faithfulness in the use of Scripture.

In 1952 Billy Graham visited the torn but victorious Korean church.

... out of grief and tragedy had come a heroic church, whose people know great joy in the things of Christ. If I had not believed in Christ before coming to Korea, I would have been compelled to believe that a Christian is different. These people had a joy and a happiness in their faces that stood out in sharp contrast to the thousands about them.

We learned that the secret of their strength is their faithfulness in the use of Scripture. Here is a church which has been built on the Bible, where Bible reading has been born out of suffering and grief. Here is a church which is politically and materially weak, yes, but spiritually strong—probably the strongest in all the world today. Numerically the Christians in South Korea number about one and a half million, but spiritually they have the power of the early church.... we saw their faith when we visited their early morning prayer meeting in a half-built church, without sides or roof. Every morning, throughout the land, thousands crowded at five and six o'clock for an hour or two of fervent, believing prayer.

The Race Question

> . . . in the final analysis the only real solution
> will be found at the foot of the cross, where we
> come together in brotherly love.

The Christian looks through the eyes of Christ at the
race question and admits that the church has failed in
solving this great human problem. We have let the
sports world, the entertainment field, politics, the
armed forces, education, and industry outstrip us. The
church should have been the pace setter. The church
should voluntarily be doing what the federal courts are
doing by pressure and compulsion. But in the final
analysis the only real solution will be found at the foot
of the cross, where we come together in brotherly love.

If America Falls,
the Church Will Have Failed

> . . . I sent to you Timothy . . . to remind you
> of my ways in Christ, as I teach them every-
> where in every church. (I Cor. 4:17 RSV)

If America falls, it will be because the church will
have failed. It won't be the government that failed. It
won't be any other area of our society that failed. If
America falls, it will be the church's fault because the
church did not live in the spiritual atmosphere, and
breathe the heavenly air, and get into action by the
anointing of the Holy Spirit before it was everlastingly
too late.

God's Rightful Place

In a few days Ahab and Jezebel were taken from the throne and God was given His rightful place in the land of Israel.

It was a dark hour when Elijah climbed to the top of Mount Carmel—all the prophets of Baal were against him, the king and queen opposed him, the army was his enemy. He was alone! There were seven thousand people who did believe, but they were hiding in caves, afraid. Only one man dared to believe God would send a revival. Seven thousand people told Elijah, "It can't be done. Everything and everyone are against you!"

People, often God's children, say the same thing today. Let me tell you that nothing is too hard for God!

But they had a revival in Elijah's day! On top of Mount Carmel the prophets of Baal called on their god. There was no response—he was off on a fishing trip and couldn't hear them, or he had gone off somewhere else and couldn't hear. Elijah called upon God to rain down fire. The fire fell and revival came to the men of Israel. In a few days Ahab and Jezebel were taken from the throne and God was given His rightful place in the land of Israel.

Conditions of Revival

If I regard iniquity in my heart, the Lord will not hear me. (Ps. 66:18)

What are God's conditions for revival? First, realization of need and a desire for revival. I am talking to Christians now. Do you want a revival today? Would you like to see this city moved from center to circumference? Would you like God to bless us and people to turn to Him? Would you like Hollywood to be so shaken that it might influence the world for Christ? Would you like the Spirit of God in our midst as He has never been before? We can have it! I say we can have it if we meet God's conditions!

The second condition for revival is repentance. Scripture says, "If I regard iniquity in my heart, the Lord will not hear me" (Ps. 66:18). Do you know what repentance is? Repentance is renouncing sin. Many people say they believe God's Word and accept Christ's sacrifice, but they have never been truly repentant! If they were, their lives would show it.

And then the third thing is to pray. Revival never comes except in answer to prayer. A few months ago the city of Augusta, Georgia, was moved upon by the Spirit of God. Do you know why? Before we ever arrived, there were thirteen thousand prayer meetings held in that city. God was moving before we got there, in answer to prayer. . . .

Fourth, in order to have a revival we must have faith. Unbelief is a sin that keeps back revival in city after city because people will not believe God's Word and take Him at His word. God says that if we meet certain conditions, He will send a revival; He will send the blessing, and sinners will turn to Him. We have to take God at His word and not doubt Him. We need revival!

Is My Minister "Unreal"?

Think of him as a human like yourself—
needing friends.

One of the most misunderstood professionals in our society is the parish minister. With a high calling that is ordained of God, he often finds himself given only a few moments a week in which to communicate divine truth. He is urged to be relevant, but criticized if he is too contemporary.

His life style is expected to exude holiness, yet if he doesn't identify with the masses, he is too exclusive. In an age of unbelievable secular pressures, he must stimulate flagging interest in the work of the kingdom. Furthermore, he must time church services so as not to intrude on an early afternoon TV football game.

I have the greatest respect for these men and tell you frankly they are not "unreal" in any way. More than anyone else in our society, they come to grips with the issues of life and death which other disciplines have too easily ignored.

You can assist him, however. Try a kindly smile and a warm handshake whenever you meet. Think of him as a human like yourself—needing friends. Try praying for him, too. That will do wonders for both of you.

Contemporary Worship

". . . the hour is coming, and now is, when the true worshipers will worship the Father in spirit and truth, for such the Father seeks to worship him." (John 4:23 RSV)

Here's someone bugged by changes in her church's worship service: "I'm being turned off by happenings in my church. I accepted the young people playing guitars, the change in liturgies, and the increasing use of lay readers. But now, we're supposed to show friendliness by greeting others in the pews and developing a sort of party-like atmosphere. I don't like it—and wish for the old days of sedate and serene worship. What's happening?"

Billy Graham answers from his perspective:

Some churches in recent years have indeed undergone marked changes in the worship experience. For older people—I detect you are one of them—this is a difficult if not a painful experience.

But remember a couple of things. First, that the aim behind such radical developments is to simplify and enhance the act of worship. Supposedly, at least, these make man's approach to God easier and understandable, and that's a worthy aim.

Don't get hung up on the details of the change itself. Be flexible enough to cooperate—and pray before the worship hour begins that God will reveal Himself through all that is to follow.

Remember also that the Christian ought to be able to worship anywhere and under all circumstances. Fellowship with God is a spiritual relationship, which surroundings and procedures may enhance or diminish, but can never destroy.

Read the conversation that Jesus had with the woman at the well in John 4, particularly the comments on worship in Jerusalem. He helped her see that it was not something geographical, but an exercise of the spirit.

Can We Really Believe in the Church?

> . . . the husband is the head of the wife as Christ is the head of the church, his body, and is himself its Savior. (Eph. 5:23 RSV)

I presume occasionally many of us have some displeasure with the church, because the church is people and people are imperfect. But wait a serious minute! Let me make it clear I am also *for* the church. Of all the world's institutions, the Christian church stands out as the most amazing. It stands like a Rock of Gibraltar in the tides and currents of the centuries. It has produced more thought, transformed more lives, contributed more inspirational literature, has built more charitable institutions, and produced more art and music than all the rest of man's efforts put together.

The church, however, is primarily the body of Christ. The Bible says, ". . . Christ is the head of the church. . . ." (Eph. 5:23). The Bible also says that it was Christ's love for the church that caused Him to go to the cross. If Christ loved the church (the body of believers everywhere) that much, I cannot hate it. The fact is, I must love it too.

I must pray for it, defend it, work in it, pay my tithe and offerings to it, help to advance it, promote holiness in it, and make it the functional, witnessing body our Lord meant it to be. You go to church with that attitude this Sunday, and nobody will keep you away the next.

The Church—a Great, Glorious, and Triumphant Organism

> . . . within the true church there is a mysterious unity that overrides all divisive factors.

. . . the family of God contains people of various ethnological, cultural, class, and denominational differences. I have learned that there can even be minor disagreements of theology, methods, and motives, but that within the true church there is a mysterious unity that overrides all divisive factors.

In groups which in my ignorant piousness I formerly frowned upon, I have found men so dedicated to Christ and so in love with the truth that I have felt unworthy to be in their presence. I have learned that although Christians do not always agree, they can disagree agreeably, and that what is most needed in the church today is for us to show an unbelieving world that we love one another. To me the church has become a great, glorious, and triumphant organism. It is the body of Christ, and the humblest member is an important part of that body. I have also come to believe that within every visible church there is a group of regenerated, dedicated disciples of Christ.

14

Some Aspects
of the Christian Life

Billy's Call to Preach

> All right, Lord, if you want me, you have got
> me.

I will never forget one day of my three years at
Trinity College in Tampa, Florida. God was speaking
to me, but as yet I had not made my decision to go
into the ministry. That certain day Dean John R. Min-
der made a compelling appeal to us during chapel
hour. He challenged us to go out and spread the Word
of God, to give our lives to Christ. After that sermon I
knew I had to make a decision. That night I took a
walk to the Temple Terrace golf course and talked it
out with God. I felt that the Lord wanted me, but I did
not want to yield my life to Him. That personal battle
went on for hours. I walked, paused, stopped, stood
still, kept on walking. Somewhere around midnight it
was decision time. I knelt alongside the eighteenth
green, bowing my knees and my heart, and said, "All
right, Lord, if you want me, you have got me." A few
days later the postman left a letter in the mailbox of
my parents at Charlotte, North Carolina. My mother
told me later that the contents of that letter made that
day one of the happiest of her life. For seven years she
had prayed that I would make such a decision!

Christians in Politics?

The people are hungry for a moral crusade. . . .

We need good Christian men to offer themselves for political office. One reason we don't have better men in Washington is that too few Christian men offer themselves. They are afraid. They say, "We ought not to delve in politics." God didn't say that to Daniel. Daniel lived in a country far more heathen than ours, and he was prime minister under seven kings in two empires. The people are hungry for a moral crusade, and they need a Moses or a Daniel to lead them in this hour.

Soul Sleep?

I am hard pressed between the two. My desire is to depart and be with Christ, for that is far better. (Phil. 1:23 RSV)

The subject of death is getting more attention today. Many colleges and universities have courses in this subject. Too long we have winked at its presence and ignored its significance.

The Bible has a great deal to say about it, and one of its main messages is that faith in Christ has finally broken the tragic hold that death has had on all mankind. If you were to judge merely by Old Testament statements, you might think there was a sort of suspended animation at death. Paul, however, gives a later definition.

In Philippians he speaks of being "with Christ" which he says is "far better" than life here. In Hebrews 12:1, the writer certainly doesn't suggest any idea of the dead in Christ sleeping idly without consciousness, for he says they are witnesses of the race set before living Christians.

I know it is difficult to think of a conscious existence for a disembodied spirit, but the New Testament principle is simply this for the Christian: "absent from the body—present with the Lord."

Paul would not have said "to die is gain" unless he meant that what is gained in the presence of the Father more than counterbalances the loss. Death does not terminate the existence of the Christian, but gives it more freedom and a wider range.

The Gap of the Unexplainable

. . . need plus repentance plus faith equals life and hope.

This common question is asked: "I happen to be one of those people who can't believe in anything not scientific. That means I don't believe in God. Why do we have to invent things to fill the gap of the unexplainable?"

Billy's answer is worth notice:

And I happen to be one of those people who feel we would be awfully deprived if we couldn't believe in things which didn't have scientific proof. Where, for example, would there be room for a mother's love, or an old friendship? Or, particularly, faith? I question whether you really operate on the rigid atheistic basis you propose.

As a matter of fact, the Bible says it is impossible to know God purely through the intellectual processes. If we try, we end up being ridiculous and foolish. The Bible teaches we must just "believe that He is" (Heb. 11:6).

Incidentally, I like your phrase "the gap of the unexplainable." Most people find in life so much that can't be satisfactorily explained. It is right there that faith in Christ provides an answer. I mean things like purpose for living, what is after death, and the provision for forgiveness.

If you are as loyal to the scientific method as you claim, wouldn't it be in order to check out every hypothesis, every theory? Even if you come to Christ on that basis, you will "taste and see that the Lord is good" (Ps. 34:8).

Don't miss the new life of faith just because it can't be proven in a laboratory. There are tens of millions of people throughout the world today who know God because they followed a well-proven equation: need plus repentance plus faith equals life and hope.

Quit Defending Christians

The Scripture deals with conditions "under the skin," as you put it, and it says we're all cut from the same faulty fabric. . . .

Here's an honest question: "I don't go to church because most of the church folk I know are plain hypocrites. I don't want to be one. In their finery in the sanctuary, you'd think they were God's elite. Under the skin, however, they are like the rest of us. Can you dispute that?"

Billy's answer must have jolted the one asking the question:

If I tried to dispute the fact that the nature of man is essentially sinful, I'd have the Bible against me. The Scripture deals with conditions "under the skin," as you put it, and it says we're all cut from the same faulty fabric (Rom. 3:23). The only thing is, church people who know Christ as personal Savior have let the

Lord provide forgiveness and a holy standing in the sight of God.

Perhaps the best answer for you is a quote from a letter I received. This person wrote: "I do wish, Dr. Graham, that you would quit defending Christians. We need no defense, for without the grace of God, we are just like anyone else and have nothing to boast about. Christ said, 'They that are whole need no physician,' and that sums it up. We who go to church do so because we have a need. Yes, we are hypocrites and sinners, and we admit it."

You know, once when Peter became suspicious of John and asked about his condition, Jesus said, "What is that to you? You follow me!" (John 21:22.) How is that advice for you? What a tragedy if you mock other seekers and miss finding heaven yourself!

Is Jesus Responsible for Deaths?

"You have heard that it was said, 'You shall love your neighbor and hate your enemy.' But I say to you, Love your enemies and pray for those who persecute you." (Matt. 5:43, 44 RSV)

A mother asks a curious question: "My children came home from church last Sunday saying, 'Mother, we're never going to church again. We learned that Jesus has been responsible for more deaths than any man in the world.' Now, I can't imagine who told them that—but what do you make of it?"

Billy's answer surprises the mother:

It seems to me like a distortion caused by lifting a statement out of its context.

First of all, the whole thrust of the Bible is that Jesus Christ came to give life, not death. He said this Himself in John 10:10. He also advised in Matthew 5, ". . . Love your enemies, bless them that curse you, . . .

and pray for them which despitefully use you . . . that ye may be the children of your Father which is in heaven. . . ."

What your children may refer to is some statement regarding the religious wars of history. These are tragic chapters of human experience in which many were killed for reasons of faith, sometimes perverted faith. But to charge Christ with these excesses is like charging the automobile manufacturer with what a drunken driver does with his vehicle.

Perhaps the superb demonstration of Christ's love prior to His death on Calvary's cross was His statement in Luke 23:34, "Father, forgive them; for they know not what they do." This is not the sentiment of one who deals in death.

Furthermore, it occurs to me that the best way to begin answering your children's theological questions is to go to church with them, not to send them.

Happiness

> Thou dost show me the path of life; in thy presence there is fulness of joy, in the right hand are pleasures for evermore. (Ps. 16:11 RSV)

An old Scottish author put it well when he said: "No state can be more destitute than that of a person who, when the delights of sense forsake him, has no pleasures of the mind."

I am concerned, of course, about the increasing evidence of dissatisfaction among Americans. It seems to grow in direct ratio to our increased affluence and concentration on materialism. But now, the Bible's teaching indicates this is not strange at all. Indeed it shows unhappiness tied to the disregard of spiritual truth. Psalm 16:11 has the formula. It says that at God's right hand "there are pleasures for evermore."

When our mind and heart are fixed on Christ, we develop an overarching satisfaction in life that absorbs lesser disappointments.

Career Choice

. . . put your trust in the Lord. (Ps. 4:5 RSV)

A teen-ager writes Billy: "I gave my life to Christ after one of your telecasts. What concerns me is my future. I'm just a teen-ager, but I find career choices so confusing. Can you help me?"

Billy's answer is helpful:

I want you to do two things. The first concerns your own spiritual life, and the other, the combination of attitudes and attributes with which God has endowed you.

Make your Bible-study and prayer time more regular and more intense. It is here in the statements of Scripture that the will of God starts to take shape. Some admonitions, certain stories, and a few of the statements of Christ will leap out of the context and mold themselves into directional clues for your future. The Bible deals in principles and basic concepts, and the right career for you must have these as foundation stones.

Secondly, explore in every way possible the capacities and capabilities you have so that they may be matched with possible career choices. Psychological tests of aptitude and competency are aids that point you in the right direction. Get the counsel of someone in your church congregation who understands personnel work and have periodic discussions about choices that are formulating.

Don't make premature decisions because of family or peer pressure. Seek out particularly career choices which can represent opportunities of Christian service. View life as an exciting investment which you as a good steward can make for the Lord.

Today Set Goals

> Remember too that God wants you to move ahead even more than you do, and He will provide every aid necessary.

Discouragement is one of Satan's most effective weapons. Don't let the vast vistas of Christian growth intimidate you by their size or complexity. The Christian life is essentially a gradual growing experience. It's all in an environment of love where God is an understanding Father and Christ is an elder brother.

Remember also the importance of the beginning steps, no matter how small they may be. Job once said, "Though thy beginning was small, yet thy latter end should greatly increase" (8:7).

My suggestions are as follows: get active in a church where the Bible is honored and the gospel preached; resolve to read a part of the Bible and to pray each day; cultivate the attitude of dependence upon God and love for your fellow men; share your faith whenever possible; celebrate in your own life daily the joy of being a child of God.

Today is a good day to set some goals for yourself. Remember too that God wants you to move ahead even more than you do, and He will provide every aid necessary.

Realistic Optimism

> . . . The Lord is the everlasting God, the Creator
> of the ends of the earth. He does not faint or
> grow weary, his understanding is unsearchable.
> He gives power to the faint, and to him who has
> no might he increases strength. . . . they who wait
> for the Lord shall renew their strength, they
> shall mount up with wings like eagles, they shall
> run and not be weary, they shall walk and not
> faint. (Isa. 40:28-31 RSV)

I don't blame people for being pessimistic. But faith
in Christ introduces a whole new dimension to life. It's
one of hope and confidence. It guarantees that the human race will not be extinguished on some remote
beach, but will see the consummation of history as
Christ returns to become King of kings.

Here's a statement sure to produce a realistic optimism. Read Isaiah 40:28-31. Ponder well the
prophet's words which promise running without wea-
riness and walking without faintness.

What's in store? Nobody knows. But because of the
love and mercy of God, there's always hope.

The Inevitable Mood of Optimism

> . . . I will give them one heart, and put a new
> spirit within them; I will take the stony heart out
> of their flesh and give them a heart of flesh, that
> they may walk in my statutes and keep my ordi-
> nances and obey them; and they shall be my
> people, and I will be their God. (Ezek. 11:19,
> 20 RSV)

No Bible student is surprised at the gathering storm
we are seeing on every hand. In II Timothy 3:1 Paul
says that in the last days "perilous times shall come."
Most feel now they have arrived.

But now, I am an optimist, because that's the spirit of the Bible. It's a book that opens with splendor amid the holy courts of God and closes on the same beautiful note. In between, of course, are the episodes of human rebellion and failure, but, thanks be to God, Christ has opened the door to forgiveness and the new life of faith. That's what brings the inevitable mood of optimism.

The Will of J. P. Morgan

> J. P. Morgan was just as dependent on the cross of Christ as the dying thief.

... In the will of J. P. Morgan, the great financier of Wall Street, many dispositions were made, some of large sums of money that affected the financial equilibrium of the world, but here is what he said to his children in his will: "I commit my soul into the hands of my Savior, full of confidence that having redeemed me and washed me with His most precious blood, He will present me faultless before the throne of my heavenly Father. I entreat my children to maintain and defend at all hazards, and at any cost of personal sacrifice, the blessed doctrine of complete atonement of sin through the blood of Jesus Christ, once offered, and through that alone." J. P. Morgan was just as dependent on the cross of Christ as the dying thief.

I Have Not Been Sick One Single Day

> ... I have been very conscious of God's presence continually.

At the conclusion of a tour of India and the Far East, Billy could, by God's grace, write:
I have not been sick one single day. I do not have

any cold, sore throat, or stomachache. Everything has been absolutely perfect. I do not know where the strength has come from for the various activities that we have been called upon to do on this trip. It's really beyond me. It certainly hasn't been strength that I normally have. I just don't have this strength. It has been God's strength daily. Of course I have a great tiredness, but there has always been strength for the task. The Lord also has given me great grace in being patient with all the various responsibilities and problems that have presented themselves. In no way do I say it boastfully, but I say it to His glory. I have not lost my temper once and try to wait patiently on everybody. I have also felt something else that has been very strange, and that is an expectant faith all the time, continually believing that something is going to happen, believing that the strength will be there; and I have been very conscious of God's presence continually.

A Pitiful Yet Lovable Sight

> Let the children come to me, do not hinder them; for to such belongs the kingdom of God. (Mark 10:14 RSV)

We went out to the beach this morning and spent about an hour and a half. The little children soon came around us, most of them practically naked, but they were about as cute and sweet as anything I've ever seen. They were as black as ebony and had happy, sweet expressions on their faces. The little girls all have their noses punctured, with jewelry in the nose and in the ears. The little girls also have a lot of gold- or brass-looking ornaments on their arms.

One little boy whom we liked especially did all sorts of little dances for us. He could make all of his bones in his body crack. His arms and legs were very skinny from malnutrition, sores were on his back—he was a pitiful, yet lovable sight. As soon as we went back to the taxi, we gave two or three of them a rupee each. They went wild!

History Is Not Wandering Aimlessly

> I believe that when our Lord prayed "thy kingdom come, thy will be done in earth, as it is in heaven," He prayed a prayer which is going to be answered.

I have an increasing confidence in the ultimate triumph of the kingdom of God. I am convinced that history is not wandering aimlessly, but that there is a plan and purpose in what often seems to us hopeless confusion. God has intervened more than once in history, and there is every reason to believe that He will intervene again. Man may build his towers of Babel, as he always has, and the world may marvel at his genius and his ability to make progress even apart from God, but history shows that ultimately man comes down from his tower in confusion and chaos, disillusioned and frustrated. The Scriptures declare that there is only One whose kingdom shall never end. I believe that when our Lord prayed "thy kingdom come, thy will be done in earth, as it is in heaven," He prayed a prayer which is going to be answered. This will come about not by man's efforts within history itself, but by a direct, climactic intervention of the sovereign God.

15

Overcoming Hang-ups

A Stumbling Block

In America, in Europe, in Asia, in Africa, the cross of our Lord Jesus Christ is still a stumbling block to men who want to go to heaven but are not willing to pay the price of the cross.

In Galatians 5:11 Paul speaks: "And I, brethren, if I yet preach circumcision, why do I yet suffer persecution? then is the offence of the cross ceased."

That expression "offense of the cross" at first may sound strange to the modern mind. For we have crosses on our churches, embossed on our Bibles, and as ornaments around our necks. The cross is an emblem of art to the poets. There may be nothing wrong with this sentimentality, but the Bible teaches that the cross as understood in New Testament days was an offense, a stumbling block, a scandal to men.

Paul found that wherever he went he had no difficulty until he began to preach the cross. Wherever he went he found that the cross was an offense, a stumbling block, a scandal. People did not want to talk about it, and they did not want to hear about it. After two thousand years it has not changed. In America, in Europe, in Asia, in Africa, the cross of our Lord Jesus Christ is still a stumbling block to men who want to go to heaven but are not willing to pay the price of the cross.

Components of Problem Solving

. . . the fruit of the Spirit is love, joy, peace, longsuffering, gentleness, goodness, faith, meekness, temperance: against such there is no law. (Gal. 5:22, 23)

"I have a friend," begins this questioner, *"who has been receiving psychiatric counseling for a long time."* Then comes the stickler: *"Why is it, however, that nothing seems to change? I have accused her of merely 'handling' her difficulty rather than resolving it. How do you get off dead center in problem solving?"*

Billy's answer:

Many people turn to psychiatry and other helping professions merely to get "first aid" treatment. It seems as if after some superficial exploring of a problem, they resign themselves to their malady of difficulty and never follow through with a definite remedy.

Maybe it's because they realize the solution will require more time or more energy than they wish to give. Some get initial relief from discussions with a counselor and decide to "let well enough alone." Your friend may actually be receiving more help than either of you realize. Or it could well be that the healing process has been stalled by a lack of genuine cooperation.

In any case, continue your friendship in an atmosphere of patience, understanding, and love. Point this person to the transforming power of faith in Christ. Help her to acquire ever larger quantities of the gifts of the Holy Spirit, which Paul enumerates in Galatians 5:22, 23. They are the real components of problem solving.

Devil Worship

. . . Resist the devil and he will flee from you. Draw near to God and he will draw near to you. . . . (James 4:7, 8 RSV)

Here is a current question: "This business of Satan worship puzzles me. If seems wrong at first, but perhaps it's just a momentary diversion in a world where even religion gets monotonous. Why be so upset about it?"

Billy's answer doesn't hedge:

Satan worship is neither "momentary" nor a "diversion." It is rather a perversion that has existed from the beginning of the human race. We do well to be disturbed by it because it totally distorts this life—and damns the soul for the life to come.

The real problem now is that Satan is viewed more and more as the incarnation of man's human nature, and as such, can be rightfully deified. Nothing is further from the truth! The Devil is called various things in the Bible—the enemy, the deceiver, and the old serpent. All of them imply that his aims are always and ultimately against God and men.

Here's another reason for being upset, and this was reported recently in a popular magazine. Experts are now saying that occult practitioners leave themselves open to mental derangement, criminal tendencies, and possible self-destruction.

Don't be so nonchalant about a matter that concerns your eternal destiny. Christ has come so that through faith in Him, Satan could be defeated, hell avoided, and heaven gained. The apostle James says in James 4 that there's only one thing to do with the devil, and that's "resist him."

Secular Humanists

> . . . those who live according to the flesh set
> their minds on the things of the flesh, but those
> who live according to the Spirit set their minds
> on the things of the Spirit. (Rom. 8:5 RSV)

*Disturbed, a questioner asks Billy Graham what he
thinks of a man on TV who expressed opposition to
God.*

Billy says:

That actor may have been one of a growing group of
secular humanists. These are they who in error teach
that our total obligation is limited to the welfare of
mankind. They say we can perfect our natures without
the aid of divine grace. History is littered, however,
with the tragedy of people who have discovered too
late that within themselves lies no hope.

Organized religion as such may be throttled in the
days ahead in America, but a personal faith in Christ
cannot be destroyed. It shines best in the darkest
places.

Prejudice

> . . . I don't believe the Bible permits us to view
> any race as inferior.

*Here's a crucial question: "I am deeply concerned
about my mother-in-law. She claims to be a Christian
and yet has a great deal of prejudice. It is rapidly getting to the point where I won't be able to visit her because I stay upset for weeks afterward. My husband
gets very defensive if I discuss this with him. What can
I do?"*

Graham's convictions come out in his answer:

The first thing is to continue fighting prejudice in your own life. God has helped you to resist that evil, and hopefully your good attitude will influence others.

Your husband sounds more defensive about his mother than her prejudice. I know he's in a difficult position, but if he has maturity and integrity, he will stand with you in what is right. The dictionary calls prejudice "irrational hostility." It is also un-Biblical because I don't believe the Bible permits us to view any race as inferior.

You have a hard assignment. You will have to associate with someone who has a rather basic disagreement with you, and yet you cannot be suppressed in your own viewpoint. Pray for your mother-in-law that the "eyes of her understanding" might be opened and that Christ's love might drive out this unfounded bias. Let God give you extra love and understanding because, of course, you can't isolate those with whom you disagree.

Prejudice is everywhere evident in our world. You find it between the Arabs and the Jews, the Pakistanis and the Indians, the Chinese and the Koreans. But wherever it appears, it is an insult to the God who, having loved the whole world, sent His Son to prove it.

Gambling

. . . we are stewards of God . . . all God has given us is a trust. . . .

I've often heard parimutuel gambling defended on the basis that most of the profits are given back to the bettors or invested in some worthy cause. However, this is hardly sufficient to commend it.

Actually, gambling is one of the oldest and most devastating sins. Aristotle and Confucius denounced gamblers who by superior skills victimized their innocent patrons. I denounce it on the ground that we are stewards of God and that all God has given us is a trust to be protected and invested for God's glory and man's welfare.

How much better it is to trust God and not lady luck! Let's face it—happiness and success really come to us through honest toil and genuine faith. To trust in chance is neither Biblical nor logical.

Gambling is also disqualified since it is a violation of the commandments "Thou shalt not covet" and "Thou shalt not steal."

It is argued that people will gamble and that the state may as well have the revenue. Former governor Thomas E. Dewey said: "It is fundamentally immoral to encourage people to believe that gambling is a source of revenue. The history of legalized gambling in this country and abroad shows that it has brought nothing but poverty."

Talk about a sure thing, how's this from II Corinthians 2: "Thanks be to God who *always* causes us to triumph in Christ."

Middle Age

> If any of you lack wisdom, let him ask God, who gives to all men generously and without reproaching, and it will be given him. (James 1:5 RSV)

Here is a gut-level question: "I'm sick of being reminded of the problems of the very young and the very old. The intimation is that those in the middle-age group have little to worry them. I know differently, and I wish someone somewhere could provide some help. Why doesn't the church say more about our age group and stop taking us for granted?"

Billy's answer is helpful:

I am aware of some churches who have done exactly what you suggest. In one case, it is a special Sunday school class that relates itself to the problems of the middle-aged. They talk about such things as rearing problem children, getting along with in-laws, employment security and job challenge, plus the inevitable downward trend of life goals in the middle years.

In another church, group therapy sessions have been arranged, using the services of a local psychologist. Insights come through mutual sharing of problems and solutions, and the comparison of Bible teaching.

The marvel of the Scripture is that it has something for everyone. Are you aware of God's promise in Isaiah 46:4, where He asserts that even to old age He will carry and sustain His own? It was said of Jesus in John 2:25 that nobody needed to tell him of the changing needs of human personality, for "He knew what was in man."

Do what you can at the human level to air your problem and find solutions, but remember above all that James has promised that if we lack wisdom, God will give it to us, liberally and without criticism (1:5).

Sources for Readings

The Holy Spirit
"Filled with the Spirit"—in Charles T. Cook, *The Billy Graham Story* (Van Kampen, 1954), pp. 100-101; "The Spirit of God Lives in You!"—*The Jesus Generation* (Zondervan, 1971), p. 151; "The Unpardonable Sin"—Chicago Tribune-New York News Syndicate [hereafter CT-NYNS] (1974); "The Power of the Holy Spirit"—in *The Billy Graham Story*, p. 21; "The Holy Spirit Will Help"—*The Jesus Generation*, pp. 151-52; "A Time for Self-examination"—in *The Billy Graham Story*, p. 101; "Rely Constantly on the Holy Spirit"—*Peace with God* (Doubleday, 1953), pp. 163-64; "Supernatural Power Without the Fullness of the Spirit" —*Revival in Our Time* (Van Kampen, 1950), p. 109; "The Fruit of the Spirit"—*Revival in Our Time*, p. 108; "Something Dangerous"—*Revival in Our Time*, p. 119; "Members of the Church Filled with the Holy Ghost"—*Revival in Our Time*, pp. 78-79.

Sex
"Sexual Liberties While Engaged?"—CT-NYNS (1973); "Premarital Sex?"—CT-NYNS (1973); "Homosexuality" —CT-NYNS (1974); "Sex Placed Before American Young People"—*Revival in Our Time*, p. 72.

Marriage
"Common-law Relationships"—CT-NYNS (1973); "Communication in Marriage"—CT-NYNS (1974); "I Forgave ... But I Can't Forget"—CT-NYNS (1974); "Stepping Out on My Wife"—CT-NYNS (1974); "The Importance of Marriage"—CT-NYNS (1974); "Adultery"—CT-NYNS (1974).

The Family

"Phasing Out the Family?"—CT-NYNS (1974); "An Illegitimate Child"—CT-NYNS (1973); "Family Interpersonal Relationships"—CT-NYNS (1973); "An Effective Testing Ground"—CT-NYNS (1973); "Radicals"—CT-NYNS (1973); "The Child and His Home"—CT—NYNS (1974); "TV Programs and Twelve-Year-Olds"—CT-NYNS (1974); "Childless?"—CT-NYNS (1974); "Raising a Family"—*Revival in Our Time*, p. 102; "And When He Is Old . . ."—*Revival in Our Time*, pp. 102-3, "In Dad's Steps"—*Revival in Our Time*, pp. 101-2.

Money

"I Wanted to Give"—in George Burnham, *To the Far Corners* (Revell, 1956), p. 21; "Tithing"—CT-NYNS (1973); "Money and Our Children"—CT-NYNS (1973); "A Christian View of Spending"—CT-NYNS (1974); "Making a Quick Buck"—CT-NYNS (1974); "Is Tithing Obsolete?"—CT-NYNS (1974).

Guilt, Worry, Fear, Loneliness, and Identity

"Identity Crisis"—CT-NYNS (1974); "The Fellowship of Fear Is Universal"—in *To the Far Corners*, p. 118; "Why Worry?"—CT-NYNS (1974); "I Feel So Guilty"—CT-NYNS (1974); "Rationalizing Wrongdoing?"—CT-NYNS (1974); "Age of Anxiety"—CT-NYNS (1973).

Hostility, Temper, Dissatisfaction, and Cynicism

"Cynicism Can Throttle Your Hope"—CT-NYNS (1973); "How to Handle Dissatisfactions"—CT-NYNS (1974); "Hostility to God"—CT-NYNS (1974); "Temper"—CT-NYNS (1973); "Temper"—CT-NYNS (1974).

Prayer, Piety, and Practice

"Earnest Prayer"—in *The Billy Graham Story*, p. 99; "The Power of Prayer"—in *The Billy Graham Story*, p. 20; "Holy Living"—in *The Billy Graham Story*, p. 97; "Saying One Thing, Doing Another"—CT-NYNS (1974); "It's Hard to Be a Christian"—CT-NYNS (1974); "How to Handle Adversity"—CT-NYNS (1974); "Coping"—CT-NYNS (1974); "Work"—CT-NYNS (1973); "Winning Daily Victories over Temptation and Sin"—*The Jesus Generation*, p. 151; "To the Cross with Him"—in Robert O. Ferm, *Persuaded to Live* (Revell, 1958), p. 20; "The

Joy of God on Their Faces"—in *To the Far Corners*, pp. 266-67; "A Formula to Regulate Attitude and Actions" —*Nation's Business* (September 1969), p. 49; "Wheat and Tares"—*The Christian Century* (17 February 1960), p. 189.

Christ

"Risen!"—*Revival in Our Time*, p. 142; "All of Hell Laughed"—*Revival in Our Time*, pp. 139-40; "Let This Cup Pass"—*Revival in Our Time*, p. 138; "The Purpose of the 'Silent Years' "—CT-NYNS (1974); "The Deity of Christ"—CT-NYNS (1973); "Obey Christ"—in *To the Far Corners*, p. 150; "East and West—in *To the Far Corners*, p. 145; "Heaven's Best and Earth's Best"—*Look* (7 February 1956), p. 51; "The Cross and the Resurrection"—*The Christian Century* (17 February 1960), p. 188.

Salvation

"What Is the 'Heart'?"—CT-NYNS (1974); "Is the Judgment Day Coming?"—CT-NYNS (1974); "Mental Illness and Conversion"—CT-NYNS (1973); "God Is at Work"—*Christianity Today* (13 September 1974), p. 4; "The Wrath to Come"—*Christianity Today* (13 September 1974), p. 7; "The Gospel Is . . ."—*Christianity Today* (13 September 1974), p. 8; "Businessmen Ask a Question" —*Nation's Business* (September 1969), p. 49; "This Hour of Crisis"—*The Christian Century* (17 February 1960), p. 189; "The Hero and Idol of My Heart"—*Billy Graham Talks to Teen-agers* (Zondervan, 1958), p. 11; "What Can I Do with My Load of Sin?"—*The Jesus Generation*, p. 145; "Salvation and Our Emotions"—CT-NYNS (1974); "All Have Sinned"—*Revival in Our Time*, p. 128; "Confession of Sin"—in *The Billy Graham Story*, p. 96.

The Bible

"The Origin of Prophecy"—CT-NYNS (1974); "The Bible Is The Word of God"—*Christianity Today* (15 October 1956), pp. 5-7; "The Bible's Authority Creates Faith"—*Christianity Today* (15 October 1956), p. 6; "When the Sun Shines on the Bible"—CT-NYNS (1974); "Christ, Surrender, and the Bible"—CT-NYNS (1974); "The Bible and Heaven"—CT-NYNS (1974); "The

Power of the Word of God"—in *The Billy Graham Story*, p. 21.

God's Love, Care, and Holiness

"The Holiness of God"—in *The Billy Graham Story*, pp. 95-96; "The Atomic Power of God"—*Revival in Our Time*, pp. 146-47; "Does God Know About Our Loss?"—CT-NYNS (1974); "God's Care"—CT-NYNS (1974); "The Last First?"—CT-NYNS (1973); "God Loves You"—in *To the Far Corners*, p. 148.

The Church

"Out of Grief and Tragedy, a Heroic Church"—in *The Billy Graham Story*, p. 55; "The Race Qeustion"—in *The Billy Graham Story*, p. 55; "If America Falls, the Church Will Have Failed"—in *The Billy Graham Story*, p. 95; "God's Rightful Place"—*Revival in Our Time*, p. 76; "Conditions of Revival"—*Revival in Our Time*, pp. 77-78; "Is My Minister 'Unreal'?"—CT-NYNS (1974); "Contemporary Worship"—CT-NYNS (1974); "Can We Really Believe in the Church?"—CT-NYNS (1973); "The Church —a Great, Glorious, and Triumphant Organism"—*The Christian Century* (17 February 1960), p. 188.

Some Aspects of the Christian Life

"Billy's Call to Preach"—in *The Billy Graham Story*, p. 29; "Christians in Politics?"—in *The Billy Graham Story*, p. 100; "Soul Sleep?"—CT-NYNS (1974); "The Gap of the Unexplainable"—CT-NYNS (1974); "Quit Defending Christians"—CT-NYNS (1974); "Is Jesus Responsible for Deaths?"—CT-NYNS (1974); "Happiness"—CT-NYNS (1974); "Career Choice"—CT-NYNS (1974); "Today Set Goals"—CT-NYNS (1973); "Realistic Optimism"—CT-NYNS (1973); "The Inevitable Mood of Optimism"—CT-NYNS (1973); "The Will of J. P. Morgan"—in *Persuaded To Live*, p. 19; "I Have Not Been Sick One Single Day"—in *To the Far Corners*, pp. 154-55; "A Pitiful Yet Lovable Sight"—in *To the Far Corners*, p. 42; "History Is Not Wandering Aimlessly"—*The Christian Century* (17 February 1960), p. 189.

Overcoming Hang-ups

"A Stumbling Block"—in *Persuaded to Live*, pp. 13-14; "Components of Problem Solving"—CT-NYNS (1974);

"Devil Worship"—CT-NYNS (1974); "Secular Human-ists"—CT-NYNS (1974); "Prejudice"—CT-NYNS (1974), "Gambling"—CT-NYNS (1973); "Middle Age"—CT-NYNS (1974).

Spire Strikes the Right Chord:

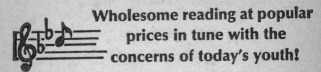

Wholesome reading at popular prices in tune with the concerns of today's youth!

Check these sure-fire hits: